Valerie

The autobiography

with Phil Gifford

Hodder Moa

National Library of New Zealand Cataloguing-in-Publication Data
Gifford, Phil.
Valerie / Phil Gifford.
ISBN 978-1-86971-262-4
1. Adams, Valerie, 1984- 2. Shot-putters—New Zealand—Biography.
I. Title.
796.435092—dc 23

A Hodder Moa Book
Published in 2012 by Hachette New Zealand Ltd
4 Whetu Place, Mairangi Bay
Auckland, New Zealand
www.hachette.co.nz

Designed and produced by Hachette New Zealand Ltd
Printed by Griffin Press, Australia
Front and back cover images: Getty

Contents

Foreword
by Sir Murray Halberg

When I look at the athletes in my day and the athletes of today there are many differences. We still ran to a tape, electronic timing had just been invented and the tracks were still cinder tracks. We had no direct assistance from the powers that be. We had coaches, but they were often not sent with teams to overseas events. There was no commercial assistance, as there is today, and barely enough money going around to send the athletes to the Games.

Today there are many different disciplines such as health, nutrition, physiotherapy and sports psychology assisting the athletes. There are all of those differences.

But some things have not changed at all. To win at the Olympic Games then, and to win at the Olympic Games today, requires the same attitude, application and commitment. And when the gun fires, or when you're called to throw, you're still by yourself. So it takes exactly the same effort, the same output, the same sort of competitiveness today as it did then — that's how it always has been and always will be.

What brings gold medal winners together and gives us that human bond, that sporting bond, is basically our love of sport and our desire to win, to be the best we can at the highest level. If we're going to the Olympics, we say, 'We don't just want to make the Olympic team, we don't just want to perform with distinction, we don't just want a medal. We want to win. We want to win. And we will not be satisfied until we're standing on the dais and we have that gold medal around our neck, and it can't be taken away.'

My association with Valerie goes right back to 2002 in Manchester, and I remember her coming into the village straight from the Caribbean where she'd just won the world junior championship. I was so impressed even then with the lady's demeanour and attitude.

Then in 2004, with the team in Athens, going to Olympia, I saw her denied the chance of being in the final rounds because the woman who led the competition was subsequently found to be a drugs cheat.

In the years since, as Valerie has been involved with the Halberg Trust and the awards, speaking at functions and meeting people, it has been a real pleasure to observe how she always gives more than is asked of her, how she puts people at ease and has such a wonderful rapport with young people.

As a competitor Valerie presents a real game face to the world, but out of competition Valerie is a big-hearted, warm and kind-natured person.

I learnt that Valerie the athlete had total focus and commitment, and you felt you shouldn't intrude on her space. She occupied her space, a space that was very powerful. I've always admired that in Valerie.

I once said that she may become our greatest athlete ever, and she could well be on track for that.

Sir Murray Halberg
Auckland, August 2012

1

Gold

My hopes for a gold medal in London all involved getting everything right in front of 80,000 people at the Olympic Stadium on 6 August 2012.

In my wildest dreams I'd never have believed the gold would come six days later, the day after the Games closed.

Nothing seemed to have changed in my world when I headed out at lunchtime on just another Tuesday to drive to my coach Jean-Pierre Egger's home in La Neuveville in Switzerland, to pick up a new pair of throwing shoes.

At 12.30 came the news that changed everything — changed my emotions, changed my life really.

It was almost unbelievable. My phone rang, and it was Dave Currie, the chef de mission of the New Zealand Olympic team. He said, 'I'm just ringing you up to let you know that the IOC has informed us that you've now won the gold medal. Ostapchuk has been done for drugs.'

I let out a massive cry. 'Are you kidding, Dave? Stop pulling my leg. Is this for real?'

He said, 'No, no, this is for real. You're now back-to-back Olympic champion.' I said I needed a moment, shut the phone off and pulled into the side of the road.

Back in Auckland, my sister Paddy had just returned a few hours before from London, and she was sound asleep when I rang. It was her husband Ken who answered the phone. I was crying, and Ken asked, 'What's the matter?'

'I've just won the Olympic Games. I've won the gold medal.'

As you can imagine, everybody in the house woke up and there was a screaming match, all of us just so happy and proud. It was such an amazing feeling.

I got myself together enough to drive, and carried on to Jean-Pierre's house. When his wife Beatrice opened the door, I started gulping and crying. She was so concerned, asking, 'What's happened? What's happened?'

I looked at her, and looked at JP, and said, 'We won, we won!'

JP walked up to me and I went into his arms and he gave me a massive bear hug. It was the most fantastic moment.

Jean-Pierre Egger

I had heard a rumour from a friend that morning that Ostapchuk had tested positive for drugs, but it was not confirmed.

When Valerie arrived, she said, 'We won the gold, we won,' and we cried.

For a minute we were all so very happy, and nobody could say one word at this time. It was one of the most fantastic moments of my life, to have so much joy.

I never dreamed something so extraordinary would ever happen in my career. Once I had heard the news I had a huge grin on my face that just stayed there for a long, long time.

The lead-in to London had been going very smoothly until just two weeks before the Games. My last meeting before London was in Lucerne in Switzerland on 17 July. I threw very well there; it could hardly have gone better. It was an awesome meeting all round. The star Jamaican sprinter Yohan Blake was competing, along with a number of other top athletes. Being in Switzerland for me was like a home competition, and they did a fantastic job staging the meeting, and the atmosphere was ideal.

At the meeting I achieved a season's best throw, and my consistency was very good, too. I actually had the best series of my career. I threw 20.72 metres, then 20.91, 21.01, 21.11, fouled, and finished with 20.86 metres.

JP and I knew we were on the right track leading into London. All the training and all the hours working on technique were paying off. Everything was going very well.

But then, on Saturday, 21 July, I hurt my back, and it was quite a bad injury. I was doing a dead lift and tore a muscle, really screwed it. I had to shut down all training for three days. On the Monday I visited specialists in Zurich and they gave me three cortisone injections.

On the Sunday I'd said to Jean-Pierre when we knew I was getting the jabs the next day, 'Have faith in me. Write the programme as you would normally write it, so we can start on Wednesday.' He asked if I was sure, and I said I was.

On Tuesday my stubborn-cow side came out and I went to the gym. On the Wednesday JP said, 'I don't know if you'll be able to get through this.' I have to admit it wasn't the easiest. I was getting physio twice a day, sometimes three or four times a day, which continued for the next five or six days.

Thank God my wonderful physio Lou Johnson was with us. She knows my back so well, and has got me through similar injuries in the past. We knew from experience that the injections would heal the back very, very quickly. Lou was scheduled to head back to London on Tuesday, 24 July, but she was able to change her flights and stay to help me.

There were times in the days straight after the injury when I was thinking, 'My God, I don't think I'm going to be able to compete at all.' But I was able to put those negative thoughts — and that's all they were, random thoughts — aside. I had faith in my ability to recover. I knew it was something that we'd encountered before, and something we'd got over completely before.

So we were able to get through the hiccup. On Friday, 27 July, I had my first throws session, and it was okay, but 10 days after the injury I was back to full sessions, throwing really well, over 21 metres, and in full swing with the weights. My mental preparation was on track as well.

We kept things quiet about the injury. I wanted to keep it behind closed doors, because we didn't need any outside pressure or speculation. By the time we flew to London on Thursday, 2 August, I was strong and dynamic again.

Three of us, Lou Johnson, Jean-Pierre and I, had taken a train to Zurich then caught a plane to London.

I was very excited heading into the village, excited about going to the Olympics, and feeling very prepared and ready to go.

I'd made a request to have a room of my own if it was possible. I wanted a little personal space to prepare for the biggest event of my life. When I got to the village I discovered that two other girls had their own rooms, but I had to share. They did offer me a single room, but it had no windows in it. JP said no to that, because it wasn't very healthy to be staying in a room with no fresh air.

They suggested Lucy Van Dalen, the 1500 metres runner, who I ended up rooming with, an amazing girl, should go into the windowless room, but I wasn't ever going to let them do that. I wouldn't have put my dog in that room.

JP just said, 'Go to the room with Lucy.' And I said okay. Don't get me wrong — it was okay after that, and Lucy was great. But I did think, 'Mmm, first little hurdle here that we didn't really have to face.'

Nick Cowan, Valerie's manager

On 9 July I got a text from Valerie, saying, 'Hi Nick, if possible could I room by myself? Could you help on this by talking with Athletics New Zealand about it as I don't want to get involved. Thanks, Val.'

I had a conversation with an official at Athletics New Zealand, saying Valerie has asked if she could have a room on her own. If she can't that's all cool, and Valerie feels that if she can't have a room on her own maybe Lucy would be good to share with as she's new and it might be helpful for her to be with someone more experienced like Val.

They said there could be a room available on her own, but it would involve a manager moving out and sharing with an athlete, which is not ideal because a manager can be getting phone calls at all hours.

I assured them that Valerie understood that, and we were only asking, so if the opportunity for a room on her own came up, could she have it please?

I texted Valerie the same night: 'Spoke about room. May share with Lucy [Van Dalen]. Still going to try for room on your own. Will keep you in the loop. Cheers Nick.'

In my mind it was a case of job done there. We didn't worry about it too much. But when Valerie got to the village two female athletes had rooms of their own. My face dropped. Val just said, 'Don't worry about it, I'm fine.'

We had a weightlifting session on the Friday. I felt really good, and there were no problems with my back.

Saturday was a day off and I went and met my sister Paddy and my niece Sharne, who'd travelled to London for the Games. I hadn't seen them since March so, as you can imagine, it was a very emotional and very happy reunion.

Meanwhile there was another strange little issue, this time over my competition uniform. I was never able to get one that fitted. If you look at my competition uniform in London I was actually wearing Nike tights with the logo removed, and not Asics, the sponsor of the track and field team.

Nick Cowan

People may wonder why getting a uniform right is important, but I'd ask: What if your wedding dress didn't fit on your wedding day? What would that do to how a bride would feel?

If you know you're on television, in front of a massive live crowd and your top is too short, or your tights are cut so they disappear into your crotch, it does have an effect.

The Asics competition uniform for Daegu, South Korea in 2011 was custom-made. Her tights didn't fit properly but she put up with it. When we signed with Toyota they used a photo of her in Daegu and the marketing manager said, 'We've just touched up the photo a little because there's a component . . . the best way to describe it would be that it doesn't help her ladylike image.'

Val keeps quiet on that. She doesn't want to rock the boat. We get a new uniform for the world indoors, in March. She throws and wins. The tights are still the way they were in Daegu — uncomfortable and embarrassing to wear.

At the end of March I told Athletics New Zealand we needed to sort things out. I kept telling them: 'Don't leave it too late. We don't want to be in a position where it's one month out and the uniform doesn't fit and we're scrambling around to get it.'

April and May came and went. We were told they were working on it with Asics, and to be fair I'm sure they were.

June comes, and we're told they're just days away. Into July and we're told they'll despatch them directly from Japan. They send them to Switzerland, where they sit in Customs for a week.

Now we're less than three weeks out, and they arrive. And when Val tries them on they're unusable, worse than the earlier tights.

We had a clause in Valerie's contract that if a suitable uniform wasn't provided in a timely fashion she could wear other clothing. So Nike, Valerie's personal clothing sponsors, found tights that would suit for London, and they resolved it in a matter of days. She got the tights three days before her competition.

What should have been a minor, straightforward issue turned into a mad scramble at the last minute.

Sunday, 5 August

At 2 pm I went online to see what pool I was in for qualifying the next morning. I had about an hour to kill before our last training session.

When I found the lists my name wasn't there. I went through it three, four, five times, but I just wasn't listed. There was no New Zealand flag in among all the other flags beside the athletes' names.

I ran into JP's room and said, 'I'm not on the start list. What do I do? What do I do?' Of course I'm in a panic because I don't know why I'm not on the list.

I started to ring people to find out what was going on.

Nobody was returning my calls, so I handed the phone over to Lou to deal with because I was freaking out.

If I wasn't on the start list I'd be sacrificing the last two years of my life being in Switzerland to do what I had to do. For an athlete, nothing could be more serious at an Olympic Games than finding you're not on the start list. That's basically a disqualification.

By a mile it was the hardest lead-up to any competition I've ever been in.

Nick Cowan

Val got Lou to ring me because she didn't feel she was getting any action. I got a text at 3.11 pm from Lou on Val's phone saying I needed to ring urgently. My first thought was an injury or an illness. When I talked to Lou and found out what had actually happened we agreed we would leave Val out of the loop while it was resolved. She didn't need to know the ins and outs.

Shortly afterwards, I talked to a team official who was with Dave Currie, and he said we're confident they'll be able to get it organised without any major difficulties. I said, 'We don't want to hear that it's being sorted, I just want honesty, and that it has been fixed, not that you're confident it'll be okay.'

Val just wanted it sorted. We never anticipated that it'd take until 7 pm to get the problem rectified.

At 3.51 pm I received a text from the same official saying we've got a meeting at 6 pm, can't do it any earlier, sorry. At 6.15 pm I sent a message saying: 'Need to know when fixed immediately and also updates, need Val to get into her pre-night routine. Please call me ASAP.' At 6.21 pm I got a text saying. 'It's been resolved. Be in touch.' At 6.50 pm a text

came, saying, 'It's live. She is in pool A. No other changes.'
Finally, at 7 pm, Val's name appeared on the start list online.

Dave Currie says he found out about the name omission before me, and if that was the case I thought he might have had the decency to tell me before I discovered it myself.

When the shit hit the fan one of the disappointing things was that my own federation, Athletics New Zealand, didn't step in. They should have been there to support me, and also to support Raylene Bates, the section manager who had not completed my entry form correctly. There weren't a lot of athletes that they had to look out for, there were only eight people in the track and field squad, and I would have expected more from them.

My whole state that afternoon wasn't good. I tried to train as well as I could, but I was only half there. The stress of having to cope with that the day before you compete means that your last training session isn't going to be easy.

I really had to knuckle down and make it through my session. I eventually got through it, but the damage had already been done. When I arrived back at the village I still wasn't on the list.

Some people might think, 'Well, she's had a lot of experience, she should be able to handle the situation.' But I've never been put in a position like this. Not being on the start list for the Olympic Games, of all events. I've never even heard of it happening to any athlete before. It's hard to deal with something so weird.

Finally, at seven o'clock my name was there. Nick and Lou had been dealing with the situation. Lou was my rock in many ways. Along with JP, she did everything she could to try to ease the stress I was feeling. It was horrible. My stomach was just churning.

Lou was the one who came in and told me I was on the start list. She was the team physio and she's been my personal physio for 13 years. She went the extra mile for me. But, really, it wasn't her job. Team management should have been a bit more proactive right from the start, when they should have been the ones to notice that I'd been left off the list.

The word was out that I hadn't been entered. In the dining hall at the village other shot-putters were asking me, 'Are you injured? Are you not able to compete? Why aren't you on the start list?'

I can understand how some people couldn't see how serious the situation was. If you were in track and field and you knew the process, you'd appreciate it more. Imagine if you've worked and saved for your dream holiday, paid for your air tickets weeks in advance, and when you got to the check-in desk the airline says they have no record of you.

So while I was glad my name was finally there, I was still nerve-wracked. I should have gone to bed and slept like a log. But my body was strung out. I couldn't get to sleep until midnight, and I was wide awake at 4 am.

Monday, 6 August

I went into the first call room at the stadium, which was all good, but when I went through to the second call room, where the formal process really begins, where you get your bib with your number and surname on it, they didn't have my name on the list or my bib printed out.

For 20 minutes I stood there and begged them, 'Please, please, check on the internet. I'm on the start list, I swear I'm on the start list, please print me a bib.'

Terrible panic, because I still didn't know, just minutes before the final call, whether I was going to be allowed to compete or not.

Eventually, after phone calls, they were prepared to print out my bib, so I could throw. It was a situation I didn't want to be in. I should have been ready, everything focused on going out there, throwing the qualifying distance, packing up and heading back to the village to get into the right space for the final.

But I was a lot more worried about just getting my name on the list. Then I had to try to regroup and focus on competing. I really had to pull myself together. I think you could see from the qualifying round the mental state I was in by then.

I didn't even get past the qualification distance with my first throw. I just threw it too early without giving it anything. In the second round I really concentrated on what I needed to do and popped out 20.40 metres. It was a strange feeling. I was blank, without the sort of feeling that I would usually have.

At the top level, my sport is a real mind game. When I won gold in Beijing I was in my zone, where you can see the attitude on my face, the 'don't eff with me, don't even bother trying to make friends with me during a competition' look. It's do or die time.

In London it was totally different. I didn't feel my usual self. It was like a bad dream, as if the person throwing in that competition wasn't me. Normally, I'm feisty, and I'm out there pushing hard, firing on all cylinders. Instead, I felt like I'd just stepped off the plane into the circle. The results I was getting didn't reflect in any way what I'd been achieving in training.

Emotions do play a massive part in your physical being when you get into a competition. If you're not emotionally there, with positive energy running through your system, it's very hard to get up. A panic attack does take a lot of energy out of you. The emotional stress will override all the physical aspects of what you've been doing leading into the competition to make sure you succeed.

The pressure meant that in qualifying I came round too early on the first throw and released too early. For the second round JP said keep down, keep low and be patient, and that's what I did.

You have three chances to qualify, and I was glad it got out to 20.40 metres, but I wasn't very happy about not getting it out there on my first round.

I headed back to the village, and tried as hard as I could to get some sleep, but my head was spinning. I badly needed to sleep, but all I could do was lie on my bed for three hours and try. It wasn't successful.

Heading into the final we prepared as normal. I always try to think positive, to get some positive energy running through the system. The stress of my name being missed from the list could have been minimised, and the omission did have some effect, but it wasn't the whole reason I threw the way I did. It was one of those situations that you have to deal with as best as you can, and I did the best I could.

There was no way the situation was completely responsible for the result. Hindsight's a beautiful thing. Maybe if I was doing it all over again I'd do my own registration — just kidding!

You can only do the best you can do on the day. But I was just not as dynamic as I normally would be. I just wasn't all there. The usual legs, the usual dynamics, were just not there. Basically, I felt like shit. I was still able to throw 20.70 metres, but it just wasn't my competition.

I tried so hard, but I just couldn't control the way I was

feeling. When I went to JP he said to me, 'Smile, Val, just try to smile. Smile and enjoy yourself out there.' For the life of me I tried, I left my heart out there trying, but it wasn't my day.

I'm sure if you saw it on television you would have seen the disappointment in my face and in my body language. It was one of those days where everything went the opposite way to what I would have wanted.

I always knew Nadzeya Ostapchuk from Belarus had the potential to throw big, but watching her throw all five throws over 21 metres was massive. In the last two months before the Olympics she was throwing some very big throws in Belarus. Anything is possible in the Games, and she just came out and did what she did.

What we'd find out, of course, was that she was cheating when she did those amazing throws. Now she's got to live with it.

Jean-Pierre Egger

I have seen what happened with Ostapchuk many times before. In our spring in Switzerland I said to Val, 'You will see that she will not start in Europe, she will not go outside her frontiers, to avoid doping control. She will come to the Games charged with drugs.'

I have seen that scenario many times in the past, and I see it is no better today in some cases. I think we have to do something about that.

I said to Val, you will have to throw 21.50 if you are to win against a doped athlete. She should make it, and we were in that shape when we left Switzerland. But all of the situations meant it was emotionally too much for Val.

I saw on the day of the competition that her face was blank, with her usual expression — very aggressive, very competitive —

not there. I knew it would be hard, and it was hard. But we must not forget that 20.70 metres is a good performance. And it is enough. In a clean competition you can win with 20.70 metres.

It took a long time to get through the mixed zone where the journalists are able to do interviews. I cried at times. A lot of tears were shed that night.

The medal ceremony was held the same night, so I cleaned up a bit, and put on a pretty face for it. After the ceremony we got taken for drug testing. Then I was able to get together with my family, and that was when the emotions really flooded out. I went back to the village really late, and tried to sleep.

Tuesday, 7 August

The next morning it was up very early to go to the Westfield press centre next to the village for more interviews, starting at 6.30 am. It was a very long day, doing the interviews, being with my family, going to Kiwi House, and catching up with Visa, Nike and Air New Zealand.

It was a roller-coaster for me. I tried so hard not to cry during the interviews at the press centre. The fact is the reporters are there to do a job, to try to get as much information as they can about what happened, and how you saw things.

But by then I think I was just a blank space. I really tried to pull it together, and I think I did okay. I had to work really hard to achieve that. To be honest, what I really would have liked to do was just curl up in bed and get over it all in private. The media people in general were pretty good with me that morning. I got a lot of support. The one that was the easiest for me was being interviewed by Michelle Pickles for TV3. Over the years Michelle's covered some big miles to report on what

I've been up to, so there's a good connection between us.

Did we prepare a public relations strategy for what I'd say? No. What came out just came out. I didn't plan anything, but I did feel there was no point in blaming people for my poor performance on the day.

At about 7.45 we moved from the press centre to a coffee shop in the Westfield mall: JP, Nick, Ashley Abbott (the New Zealand Olympic Committee's communications manager) and Margaret Webster, also from the NZOC, and me.

It was agreed that it was important we meet with Dave Currie so he could explain to me directly what had happened with the entry form. We walked about five minutes away to a breakfast room at the local Holiday Inn, which was a little more private. We met with Dave, at around 9.30, and he apologised to me for what had happened.

He told Nick and me how on the entry forms submitted by Raylene Bates for me and Lucy Van Dalen the box confirming we would be competing had somehow not been ticked. Nick and I said, 'Please don't name Raylene.' I especially didn't want Raylene named. This is a general procedural issue; it's not completely her fault, even though she was in charge of registering the athletes. I'd spoken with Raylene, and I knew that she still had a job to do with others competing, and needed to keep it straight.

Nick Cowan
At the meeting that Val, Jean-Pierre and I had with Dave Currie, and Ashley Abbott at the Holiday Inn, Dave stepped Val through how the entry debacle had played out. We talked for a while about it, and I said we wanted some accountability about the process.

I told Dave about the rooming situation, that I felt he needed to know that now, but at the moment we didn't want to talk about it publicly. He said he'd be looking at it as well.

I said, 'I feel you need to know [about the room] because both JP and Valerie at the time, separately, asked if it had been done on purpose. They don't believe that now, but it's important you know that that's where they were then.'

Val and JP had to leave at about 10.30, to go to the village and pack. Val was heading for Paris at six the next morning with Paddy and Sharne, and JP was due to leave the village. That night we all stayed in a hotel, JP and his wife Beatrice, Valerie and her family, me and my son Thomas.

After Val and JP had gone, we were joined at the Holiday Inn by Kereyn Smith, the secretary general of the NZOC, and for the next 45 minutes or so Dave, Kereyn, Ashley and I went through the issues that needed to be raised.

I suggested Athletics New Zealand should take the responsibility, but they said to me, 'No, that's not fair because Athletics New Zealand are not here to defend themselves.'

Ashley specifically asked me to support the NZOC. I said I would back them on the basis they would thoroughly investigate what happened. My understanding was that it was agreed that morning that at the press conference in the afternoon Dave would say what had happened, he wouldn't name anybody, but he would say how he had gone to a meeting with the Olympic officials and was able to get the entry list sorted.

Kereyn would speak next and she would apologise on behalf of the NZOC, and say the mix-up was going to be investigated, reassuring everyone there was going to be a process to discover where it went wrong.

I basically was going to say Valerie was humbled by the

support she was getting and that while it was a difficult situation, Valerie and I had faith that the NZOC would investigate it fairly and, meanwhile, let's just get on with the Games.

I was satisfied with what we'd agreed to, and left to meet Valerie and Margaret Webster and JP at the Stratford train station at about 11.30. We took the Javelin train for the 10-minute ride to King's Cross station, and walked to Kiwi House.

Valerie's family was there to meet her and, when she walked in, the reception was amazing. People were clapping and cheering her. It was really touching.

We had a couple of commitments before Val went back to the main area. In a more private room Valerie did a video interview with Simon Plumb from Fairfax. Minister for Sport and Recreation Murray McCully came to meet Val and it gave me the chance to fill him in on what had been happening. I told him what the impact had been on Val.

You may have seen on television Valerie then speaking to the people at Kiwi House. It was easy to see the emotional effects the stresses of the day had had on her.

We had lunch at Kiwi House and I was about to take Valerie to Nike, who are just five minutes' drive up the road. But as we were leaving, outside Kiwi House I noticed that the chairman of the NZOC Mike Stanley, Kereyn, Ashley, and Dave were all conferring.

The press conference had been called for 3 pm, and we had about 45 minutes before it started. I'd planned to stay with Val at Nike and get back about five minutes before the conference started.

But when I saw such earnest talk going on among the NZOC leaders I changed my mind. On the way to Nike I said to Valerie, 'I think it might be better to drop you off and I'll get back to the press conference.' So she stayed at Nike.

I was back within 20 minutes, and to reassure myself the earlier agreement we'd all reached still held, I double-checked with Ashley, and was assured nothing had changed. Kereyn confirmed it as well.

The first shock came 30 seconds into the press conference. Dave Currie named Raylene. Then, at the end of his statement, he said, 'Right, any questions?'

Kereyn basically wrestled the mike off him, and said her piece, then she passed it to me, and I said what I'd agreed to say.

Then questions started, and one of the early questions was, 'Who found out about this [Valerie not being on the start list], Dave?' He said, 'I found out about it at 2 pm, and Valerie found out at about 2.30 pm.'

A journalist asked Dave who had informed him. He replied, 'Somebody in management, then it came through to me.' The questions kept coming, and he continued to refuse to say who told him.

They asked me, and I said I'd heard from Val, and I believed she was the first to know.

The next weird moment was when Simon Plumb asked Dave whether it was true that Valerie didn't have a room on her own, and others did.

Dave said Valerie hadn't requested a room on her own.

Plumb turned to me and asked, 'Did Valerie request a room on her own?' Twice somebody else distracted attention from his question, which I was grateful for, because I was determined not to lie.

Simon asked a third time, and I said, 'Valerie asked me to make a phone call to the athletics team management, and she made a request if she couldn't have a room on her own maybe she could room with another female athlete.'

So she did ask for a room on her own? I said, 'We're not really concentrating on rooming arrangements this morning.'

I was fuming inside, for three main reasons.

Val and I believed that we'd agreed Raylene wouldn't be named, and without even being asked Dave named her. NZOC's recollection of the meeting was different.

And in the same meeting I'd told Dave about the rooming arrangements, and that Val had requested a single room if possible.

The press conference couldn't end soon enough for me.

At the press conference I felt Dave Currie hung Raylene out to dry, and I was really sad about that. I was even more upset to read online that Raylene's husband had revealed how disappointed and upset she was.

At the end of the day it was Dave Currie's decision to name her, and I wish that she had been given more support and help throughout the situation. Someone should have been there to support her, and I was really upset that nobody was.

I sent her a text saying, 'Hey Batesy, I'm sorry Dave disclosed your name publicly. This is something I didn't want at all. I didn't say any names or anything like that. We spoke to NZOC about the process, not personnel. We're not saying any more and hope it dies down, but sorry your name's in this. It's not really about that.'

Raylene texted a reply: 'Val, thanks for the text. I heard your interview and you spoke really well. Thank you. You don't know how distraught I was when I found out it had happened. I am so sorry for the undue stress. I haven't had a chance to sit down and give you a huge hug and say how sorry I am. Yesterday was not the time. You know how much I love and care for you, and would never want to intentionally hurt you. I know it's not about me personally, so okay. Enjoy Paris. See you when you get back.'

A mishap happened, and people should be held accountable, but I think what was done to Raylene was wrong. Why was it done? In my own opinion Dave Currie was just covering his butt. He made the decision, which I think was the wrong one. I believe what was done was very unfair.

Jean-Pierre Egger

I have never in all of my involvement with athletics, which is for over 40 years, heard of what happened with the entry list. But we should not look to victimise anyone. What is important, and Val said it very well, is we have to make sure that something like this is not possible in the future.

Wednesday, 8 August

It was always planned that after I had competed at London, I would spend two days with Paddy and Sharne in Paris. I'd been away for so long, and missed them so much, so I was really happy that I could be with them during that time, especially with everything that was happening.

Some might think I left the village having a little sooky fit, but that wasn't the case; it had already been arranged.

We went to Disneyland and then to Parc Astérix theme park, featuring the brave Gauls Asterix and Obelix, and we looked around Paris, a city I've always loved. It was the first time in Europe for Paddy and Sharne, and I wanted and needed to spend time with them.

We stayed in Paris from Wednesday until Saturday, and they flew out to New Zealand on the Saturday night. Then I went back to the Olympic village. I was so sad about them leaving; I felt a little vulnerable, a bit depressed that my loved ones had gone.

At the end of the Games it's time for partying, but the way the dates fell meant I still had a job in hand. I had a Diamond League competition in Stockholm on 17 August.

Sunday, 12 August

I flew back to Switzerland, and when I got back to Biel in the evening I was picked up from the train station by my Swiss-Kiwi family, people I've become good friends with: Royna and her daughter Rebeka. They had a little doggy bag of food for me, and we went back to my room at the Swiss Olympic Centre in Magglingen, which is on a mountain overlooking the city of Biel. I had a big cry with them when they picked me up, then we had a long chat in my room.

My first thoughts, missing my family in New Zealand so much, were that I wanted to go home, but then in the morning I had a little sleep-in, decided to soldier on, and got back into my training.

Tuesday, 14 August

After the phone call that changed everything I was on cloud nine for days. It felt surreal. To a degree I don't totally feel like an Olympic champion, because there wasn't the hype, there wasn't the moment when the anthem is played.

I don't want to waste any energy, any breath on Ostapchuk. I don't want to give her the time of day, ever. I'm glad that they caught her. It's a shame it hurts our sport, and our event, but at the same time I'm so glad that the World Anti-Doping Agency and the drug-testers are doing such a great job catching these people.

At the end of the day it's not fair play. This is the reason we talk about fair play. We put in the hours, and put in our heart and soul to be the best athlete we can be. To have someone just come in and take substances to short-cut the process is very unfair, and I don't think they should get a second chance and be allowed to come back. My attitude is that once a drug cheat is caught they should be gone forever.

As for the silver medal, it's in its box, and I'm not opening it again. I can't wait until I get the gold medal.

Thursday, 16 August

I woke up to read online that Ostapchuk was accusing me of failing a drugs test in 2005, and saying that the reason I wasn't on the start list in London was because I'd tested positive.

It wasn't a nice thing to wake up to, although I wasn't too affected because it was totally untrue. Here's the interesting thing. Not one media person rang me about it. I guess they trusted me and knew that Ostapchuk was telling barefaced lies.

Friday, 17 August

In Stockholm at the Diamond League meeting I received very warm congratulations from a lot of people, not only throwers but sprinters, coaches and managers. Everyone was genuinely pretty happy for me.

One of the sprinters from the States, Wallace Spearmon, who finished fourth in the 200 metres in London, came up to me and said, 'You knew, you knew about it, you knew about it, didn't you?' I just started laughing. Among the athletes it's almost like a joke.

My friend Cleopatra Borel-Brown, a shot-putter from Trinidad and Tobago, was so happy for me. There was a lot of warmth among the shot-putters, lots of massive hugs and kisses. It was very nice and reaffirming for me. A lot of the shot put girls are happy with what happened, because it's a step towards having a level playing field for all of us.

In the Stockholm competition I won by over a metre, throwing 20.26 metres, with four throws over 20 metres. I found a new wave of energy at the meet.

The other thrower from Belarus, Natallia Mikhnevich, who I've always really liked and got on well with, came straight up to me, gave me a huge hug, offered big congratulations, and said, 'I told you so. I'm very happy for you.'

What did she mean by that? Straight after the shot put in London Natallia had come to me and said, 'Congratulations, you won the final.'

I found her reaction very interesting. You might have expected she would be supporting Ostapchuk right or wrong, but it wasn't anything like that. It was very bizarre, but very cool at the same time.

2

The road to London

October to February: New Zealand

The time I had at home over the summer of 2011–12 was very important, not just for the training, but also for my own sanity. It flew by very quickly, and the fact was the time I spent at home was literally shorter on this occasion. The previous year I didn't go back to Switzerland until the end of March, not the end of February as I did this time.

It was good to have my coach Jean-Pierre Egger there for seven weeks with me, although the New Zealand summer wasn't too flash, so training outdoors was sometimes a case of running out between downpours.

Being at home does bring some of its own stresses. As much as I loved being able to catch up with family and friends, it was really busy. My diary was full at all times. Not only did I have to train, but there were obligations to meet with my sponsors and to catch up with officials to get the campaign in place.

In New Zealand it was a mini build-up, trying to get into competition phase, because I was doing some meetings. It wasn't a full taper, the way you do when freshening up for a world championships or the Olympics, more like an 80 per cent taper before you compete.

The first competition was in Christchurch, in the grounds of Christ's College, on 4 February. We went for a drive the day before the meet, and saw the areas worst affected by the earthquakes, and it was really sad to see what had happened. Despite watching all the news reports on TV, I didn't have a full appreciation of how badly hit the city was until I saw it with my own eyes.

It was good to give something that the public of Christchurch could enjoy, to help take their minds off everything else that'd been going on. The venue wasn't big, but it was full, and the crowd of 3000 got into the event. I did reasonably okay, throwing 20.35 metres. I hoped for more, as you do.

A week later I threw in Hamilton, at Porritt Stadium. There was only a very small crowd there. To be honest, the spectators were outnumbered by my family. I was disappointed because they had the shot put event right at the start of the meet. I felt they didn't take the opportunity to make something of it, to get the crowd going, by having it in the middle of the programme.

Fair enough, the men's javelin was prime because of Stu Farquhar, a local guy, who's a friend and a very good athlete. But I thought they might have had the two events close together, which would have been good for both of us. Instead it was more like a training session. I tried to build myself up as much as possible, but it's hard without a crowd there and no commentary winding things up. I threw 20.19 metres, which wasn't too flash.

In the break before throwing in Sydney on 18 February things started to click. In Sydney it was so much more professional, and they produced a whole different atmosphere. They pulled out the something extra that was missing in Hamilton. There were so many people there, and the commentator made everyone aware of what was happening in the field events on the infield, as well as on the track.

It was awesome. It gets the hype going, which is what you want from competition. Training day in, day out is basically the same thing, the same feeling. When you go to a competition you want to have something more. I managed to throw 20.67 metres, the best of my southern summer.

March: back to Switzerland, world indoor champs

Emotionally, I found it much tougher to leave my family behind this time than it had been the previous year. I'd come over the year before thinking I was going to be back in New Zealand in July. This time I knew I wasn't going to be back until early October. So that was hard. There were tears a week before I left. If I even talked about going, I'd cry.

When I was getting on the plane, knowing that I wouldn't be having the human-to-human touch of the last couple of months, I couldn't stop texting. They told me to close my phone down in the end. It was as if I wanted that last contact while I was in New Zealand. On the plane all you can do is think and cry and try to get into a better head space.

When I got back to Switzerland the busy time at home seemed to catch up with me before the world indoors. The jet lag and everything just hit me. The realisation comes that you're in for the long haul now. When I arrived it was snowing and cold.

My fatigue from New Zealand caught up with me. But I had no choice over what I'd done. When I was at home it was the only chance I had had to do the things that needed to be sorted out, and the personal things I wanted to do.

I really had to try to get myself up for the world indoor

championships in Istanbul, on Saturday, 10 March. I had only four days in Magglingen before I took off. I had to be in Magglingen, try to get into a routine straight away and train as much as I could leading into the comp.

It was a small team that headed to Istanbul. Mike McGuigan, who runs Jean-Pierre's programmes for me in New Zealand, was the team manager, JP was the coach, and I was the only athlete.

When we got to Turkey the jet lag really hit me. I tried but I couldn't feel anything, I was out of it. I always try to have an upbeat attitude, so I didn't spell it out. JP could see it, but I was putting on a happy face, being rah-rah-rah, which has always been my approach.

I loaded up on the coffees, had good food, working to get myself going, getting as much rest as possible. I actually trained reasonably well on the Friday when we did a tonification session, a sharpening-up session in the weights room.

The morning of the competition I woke up feeling okay. The qualifying was in the morning, with the final in the afternoon.

The fact I'd finished second in the world indoors to Nadzeya Ostapchuk in 2010 wasn't completely out of my mind. I was aware there had been a lot of attention from the media in New Zealand about the fact that the 2010 indoors was the first time in over two years that Ostapchuk had beaten me. It was a little bit on my mind, but the biggest thing was making sure we got this Olympic year off to a good start.

The indoor title was where it began for me. The world indoors was one of the stepping stones towards London, and winning was important to make the mark, to draw the line in the sand about where I was this year.

We competed in the Atakoy Arena, a velodrome with a 200 metres indoor track, and warmed up next door in a basketball stadium, very similar to the one the Breakers have on the North Shore in Auckland.

Imagine all these athletes trying to run, stretch, sprint and hurdle, and with a shot put circle, too, all in this small space — it was hell. Trying to find space to do even the smallest thing was hard, but you had to roll with it. If you tried to run there was a chance, if you weren't very careful, you'd bump into someone.

They'd overheated the warm-up area so much we were all sweating just sitting down. Outside it was cold, so you went from a heated hotel into the cold and then back into an oven again. There was still a call room, just as you have with an outdoor meet, but obviously the space is a lot smaller.

I'd actually thrown pretty well at the last indoor championships, but Ostapchuk had a very good day, throwing 20.85 metres with her last throw. I didn't lose by much, throwing 20.49 metres, and getting over 20 metres five times.

I'm not making excuses, but I never compete indoors, except at the world championships. It does make a difference. I've only thrown indoors three times in my life, and they were the last three world champs. The Americans and the Europeans all have indoor competitions. Not long before the worlds in Istanbul, Ostapchuk threw 20.70 metres indoors in Belarus.

They don't drop in a concrete slab for an indoor meeting. The surface is wooden. So it's going to be faster and you have to get used to moving on the surface very quickly. The speed on every circle is a little different. On concrete you have to work just a bit harder, because the surface is rougher, whereas a wooden surface is as quick as hell. As a rule, the first throw I have in the circle at an indoor meeting is actually in competition. I don't throw the day before a competition, so there are no trial runs.

The whole atmosphere is different as well. It can feel a little confining, almost claustrophobic, compared to throwing outdoors.

Qualification isn't too difficult, because I don't put in 100 per cent, just enough to get over the qualifying mark. I felt the pressure during the warm-ups, and it was a little more difficult to get the body going, but I just did enough to get over the qualifying mark.

When we headed out for the competition itself there was a packed crowd, because a Turkish girl was running.

There's a very different feeling for the indoors. The world indoors is important, but there's nothing like the buzz there is for the world outdoors, where you can have 80,000 people in a stadium. The indoor championships feel more like a Diamond League event.

It's a world title, and you don't want to disrespect the title itself, but I think because physically the arena is so small, and not all the events are being staged (have a javelin throw inside and there could be dead spectators), and you're not in a big team, it almost feels like the Diamond League. It's very important, but the hype is not as exciting as a world champs outdoors.

Ostapchuk opened with 20.20 metres, and I fouled in the first round. When I look back there was a tiny part of me early on that was thinking, 'Please don't let it be déjà vu.' And there was an even smaller part, maybe one per cent, that was feeling, 'Maybe it's sort of okay if I finish second.'

Just that moment I was thinking, 'I feel like crap,' and I can't underestimate her. But then I switched that off, and went back to the competitive instinct, where I wanted to smash her.

In the second round I threw 20.48 metres, and I kept the lead going for the next three rounds. But I knew that at any time she could close up on me, so I kept my eye on what was going on.

Every throw against Ostapchuk has to be good. The thing with her is that she can have four crap throws and then just smack one out. That's how she operates. You have no idea at all what's she's going to do. When the shot leaves her hand you're thinking, 'Please fall down, hit the ground *now*.'

By now she was firing, and had a big throw in her last round. I was hanging out for the distance to go up, and she got close, with 20.42 metres. I didn't show anything, but inside there was a sigh of relief, because I knew I'd won. Then I got ready for my last shot and I threw 20.54.

If you just saw the brief results on paper it might have looked like a comfortable win, but it was actually one of the toughest competitions for me. There was physical fatigue, mental fatigue and emotional fatigue. It was hard going.

My main emotion after the win, big time, was one of relief. I just jumped up and down, and couldn't stop smiling.

After the competition my friend Sandra told me that she and Mike had never seen Jean-Pierre so nervous. He'd turned to them and said, 'Is Valerie jumping around because she's won, or because of what she's thrown?'

Afterwards he asked me what I was celebrating. Was it because I'd won, or because of what I'd thrown? He just wanted to make sure. I said because I'd won.

'Good, because you threw like shit.'

'I know. I just felt really tired. But I'm just so happy we won.'

'Yeah, that's our goal.' He said he could see that I was tired, and he was very happy for me to have won.

It was the first time he'd been there for a world title, and it was just great to share it with him. It's interesting to see how, when you win, at first the performance is not the main thing on your mind, just the winning. But I did soon think about both.

There was relief about having won, but at the same time there was some disappointment about what I'd thrown.

The last throw felt technically the best; I felt my left leg blocked in. I should have got into gear earlier. It was a bit like the world championships in Daegu, South Korea in 2011, when I took the lead on the fourth round. In Istanbul I had the lead earlier, but it was so narrow.

They had a medal ceremony and played the New Zealand anthem. Out of nowhere I saw this Kiwi guy who called out, 'Kia kaha bro' and waved a New Zealand flag. That was really cool, because wherever you are in the world there are always some random Kiwis — who you may or may not know — who just appear.

The medal ceremony was where I could really feel the relief. I was glad the competition was over and was obviously glad to have won.

Jean-Pierre gave me a week off after Istanbul, and I went to Paris and had a rest to recharge. I let myself be a kid again by going to Disneyland outside Paris. That was really good, and by the time I got back to Switzerland I was rejuvenated and ready to train again.

When I was in Paris I had a craving for chocolate. I don't know what it was, but for breakfast, lunch and dinner, all I ate was chocolate. I didn't backslide altogether. No alcohol at all, not a drop, but lots of chocolate. I got little fun-sized packs so that I wouldn't feel so guilty. But the thing was, instead of one big block, I was eating five or six small ones.

I had the best time there, feeling rested and happy. I still had to do three weight sessions in Paris, which weren't enough to lose all I'd gained, but mostly it was a great break.

The first training session back in Magglingen I walked in and warmed up waiting for JP. He came in, walked up, smiling as always, gave me kisses on the cheek, one, two, three, the way the Swiss do it.

He looks at me, then pats me softly on the cheeks, with the big man hands, and says, 'You're a little bit round there.' I could only say, 'Yes, you're right.' He says, 'I think maybe you've put two kilos on.' What could I say but, yes, he was right? I'd actually weighed myself before he'd turned up.

He said, 'That's okay.' He'd seen it immediately, but he was happy at the same time, because I'd taken the time to relax. I swear, within seven days all that stuff came off, and I was the same weight I was before I went to Istanbul. No more mini chocs; back to Bircher muesli, meat and rice. When the weight was off JP smiled and said, 'Yes, now you look better.'

March to May: base work and Rome

We went back into base work, which gave me three months of training before the Diamond League meeting in Rome on 31 May.

I have to say it was probably the longest three months of my life, because while the first month of training was fine, I did reach a point where I started to feel as though I couldn't see the light at the end of the tunnel.

The base training is pretty intense. We do three blocks of training, getting slightly lighter with each one.

The only break from Magglingen was for a week over Easter, when we went to Leukerbad, about two hours' drive away, where JP has an apartment. Everything had closed down at Magglingen. Leukerbad, known for its thermal baths, is where JP and Werner Gunthor did a lot of their training back in the day.

JP was a sports director at a centre there. It was snowing, minus five degrees, and so obviously we trained indoors.

We came back and continued the rest of the build-up in Magglingen.

The heaviest training was in the first two months and then there was a slight easing, sharpening up in the last month. I did lots of personal bests with overhead throws with the 4 kg and the 5 kg, and there were lots of personal bests in the gym.

Before 31 May, JP had goals that he wanted me to achieve, like maxes for three reps with the weights. I had quite a lot of personal bests, so my strength levels had shot up, along with my dynamic levels, and my athleticism had also improved quite a bit.

Everything was on track to throw well in Rome. The technique was going pretty well, we'd been working on some stuff there, so it was just a matter of bringing it all together. But you never know how the first competition is going to go because you haven't competed for so long. There's usually a teething period for that first comp, getting into the zone.

Jean-Pierre came with me to Rome, which was very good. It was important this year that he come to as many comps as possible, because we haven't had that much coach–athlete experience together at a competition. It was important that we got that experience before London. In 2011 he had come to Oslo and to Zurich for the Diamond League meets. This year he was at all three meets in New Zealand, in Rome and at the last two before London.

When you're in competition it's different from training together, and you need to know how the other functions under different kinds of pressure. For example, in a competition I don't talk much. I put my headphones on and I don't talk to anybody. It's selfish in a way, but you have to do what works for you.

We flew into Rome two days before the competition. Two days before the comp is always my rest day. We settled in at the hotel, and while JP went to see a friend I just hung out at the hotel.

It was very hot, which I like. The day before the competition the morning was free, and in the afternoon we had to train. I asked if JP wanted to kill a couple of hours at the Vatican. We were only 10 minutes away by taxi, so we arrived and, believe it or not, the Pope was there, driving around St Peter's Square in his little Popemobile. We thought what great timing it was to be able to see him. That was a great start to the day.

After lunch we went to training, which went really well. We did tonification, which is a French term that basically means toning up the muscles.

We were located next to a juvenile prison, and the track is where the prison guards and the local cops do their exercises. The big gates and electrified fences were right next to the track.

I had my lifting shoes next to my bag ready to go to the track, but somehow I got sidetracked and left them behind, so I had to do my lifting in my running shoes. At first I was a bit nervous, but JP was relaxed. He just smiled and said, 'Oh, we try, we try.' Sometimes I get the idea in my head that if I don't have the right equipment I won't be able to do what I want to.

But in fact it went better than I expected, which was really satisfying. Those little stresses are easier to handle with someone else there. Being the first competition it's easy to get a little edgy. But being JP he was very calm and collected. When I did my first lift he just went, 'Yep, go up, more weight.' He knew I could do it, and with his help I was able to be confident, too. So we got tonifying out of the way, and I had a quiet night at the hotel.

The day of the comp was really hot, around 30°C. I followed my usual routine: a late breakfast at about nine, lunch at about one, and then trying to get a nap between one and three. There's no qualifying for Diamond League, so we went to the track and hung out for an hour or so and then start warming up.

By the afternoon it was as hot as hell. We competed at the stadium they used for the 1960 Olympics. For a New Zealander it's a special place because Peter Snell and Murray Halberg won gold medals there in the 800 and 5000 metres on one afternoon.

It also meant a lot to Jean-Pierre. He told me, 'Last time I was here [in 1987] Werner [Gunthor] won a world championship with 22.23 metres.' Then he laughed. 'But you don't have to throw 22 metres today.'

The whole set-up is amazing. The main stadium has been refurbished somewhat since 1960, but the warm-up track is still the same.

When you walk in, it's a little bit like walking into Olympia in Greece, site of the ancient Olympics. Right around the warm-up track there are statues, as there are in Olympia. It feels a little like being transported back to ancient times.

When you walk into the main stadium there's a roar from the spectators. They have big gates up to keep the fans off the pitch for the soccer games that are held there. Italian crowds are crazy, in a good-natured way. They love track and field and they scream their heads off.

It's always a help to have a local person in your event, because the crowd gets even more involved, and we had Chiara Rosa, who qualified for the Olympics, so it was very exciting for her fans.

There was no indication that I was going to have a really

good series. My warm-up was rubbish, taking more throws than normal. When I went to take my first warm-up throw in the stadium I couldn't see Jean-Pierre. He'd left me at the warm-up track, and walked around to come into the stadium.

The problem with meets in Italy is that the organisation isn't very good. There are people standing around thinking they're in charge, but in fact nobody really knows how to get from A to B.

I do my first warm-up and Jean-Pierre pops up behind the circle. He's supposed to be on the side of the circle where the 100 metres start is. I look up and mime for him to look. He signals back to push my hips further in and be a bit more dynamic off the back. We give the thumbs up that we've understood each other.

Then I wait for him to reappear where he should be. But he doesn't appear. Fifteen minutes go by and he's still not there. I want him to have a look, offer some advice, because he's got such a great eye for the shot.

Twenty minutes go by, and he's still not there. So I have my last warm-up throw, and it goes okay, so I think, 'Stuff it. Let's just go for it.' When they get us in a row, and they announce my name, I still don't see him. Now I'm really wondering what the hell's happened.

I go back and start to prepare, and I look over and there he is, coming down, trying to get my attention, and signalling for me not to worry.

We get into the first round and I throw 19.61 metres, trying to push it too fast, premature release. The second throw was 19.85, but the third throw was when I felt something big was going to happen. I had so much tension in my hand but I didn't use what was there, and it still felt real big. I'd just let it come out, and it went 20.04 metres.

I thought, 'Okay!' I had the lead by then. Jean-Pierre was just saying, 'More dynamics off the back.'

The problem with getting everything right technically is that usually it's a general problem not a single issue. Where you win is with your legs. If you're a little stressed you start to rely on your upper body. So I went into my fourth throw thinking, 'Come on now, get into a good position, balancing over the back.' As soon as the shot left my hand I knew it was big. It felt big, I saw it fly, and when it landed I had the same excited reaction I'd had in Daegu, when I threw over 21 metres.

I looked over at Jean-Pierre and he was happy. I was just hoping it had cracked 21 metres, and when the distance came up at 21.03 it was the most amazing feeling.

Then I had a premature moment again with 20.14 metres, and I was saying to myself, 'Come on mate, you've got to get a good back-up on this one,' and I popped out the last one at 20.89 metres. I was thrilled, so pleased with how it had gone. Of course, the others hadn't thrown very well, with not one of them making over 20 metres, but for me it was one of the best competitions I've ever had.

A lot of people were surprised that Lijiao Gong, the Chinese girl, went past Ostapchuk. I was just happy that I'd won, and had a good series.

When I'd finished, and they had had the winning ceremony, I finally caught up with Jean-Pierre and he told me what had gone on. He said he had never, in 40 years of international athletics, ever had this problem. They wouldn't let him in. They didn't know where he was supposed to go to. He had all his accreditation, but this was Italy, and very much a case of too many chiefs and too few Indians. I also think if you're a man in a Latin country it's sometimes a little more difficult to get an answer. It took him 40 minutes to get to where he wanted to be. He's not a man who gets angry, but he said he was almost ready to wring somebody's neck.

But he was very pleased with the result, and I was happy because it was the first time, ever, that a coach has been there while I've thrown 21 metres, actually there to celebrate. In the last three years with my coach Kirsten Hellier, every time I threw a personal best, sadly she wasn't there.

What JP and I worked on, in training in the last six months, had come together, and now we knew we just had to perfect what we'd been doing.

In 2011 it was the basic stuff, and for Jean-Pierre that was enough. It was like trying to tell a kid to do 20 things, and they'll remember only two things. Now I could remember the two things, and we could go on to get more into detail, and get the extra bit more.

Jean-Pierre had been there at every step in training. The other people in the team are great, but JP is the only one who understands everything from a technical point of view.

As a kid you're looking to improve your throw by 30 centimetres or half a metre, but the aim of the game in 2012 is to make the goal for every competition a win. By how much shouldn't matter, although it does, but the real goal is to win your competition, and to make sure that you're on top of your game against everybody.

Now we're getting to the finer details of the throw. It can be frustrating at times, because you try, you try, and because shot putting is such a short and fast movement, if you're tired it'll take a toll on you, and you're not going to throw as far, and you're not going to throw as dynamically as you normally do.

Sometimes it's hard for me to accept that, because I want so much, and so much more.

JP is able to look and say, 'There's still more there,' which is very comforting, because the amount of time I've been in the sport, 13 years, the improvements are not going to be massive. This is the hard part of my career. You're only going to tweak little bits at a time. Sometimes as an athlete you get greedy, but you just have to be patient.

Jean-Pierre is great because he brings such reality to things if I'm struggling a little. 'You know, sometimes it's good to have a session like this. You must remember the session we did yesterday, so now your body is a little bit tired. This is a phase we're going through. We must come down before we come back up.' Having acknowledged that, when it does go right, it's an amazing feeling.

What we've worked on with the technique side of things is hard mentally, and sometimes physically frustrating, because you're asking your legs to move, and your body to hold, but sometimes they don't, so you just have to keep working at it.

Jean-Pierre knows there's that little bit more there that's going to make a difference. Ten centimetres in the circle is going to make half a metre's difference out there. You're working to keep the shot 10 centimetres back, as opposed to three or four centimetres, so you get that extra length of throw.

They are just little things that might sound small and easy to correct, but they're not. They're actually difficult. You're not a robot, but you're trying to make your body act like a robot, trying to reproduce a certain throw again and again and again. That's where the frustration is. Out of five throws you might have one or two that are okay, one or two that are good, and one that's great. You try to make them all great.

This year it's like a step forward — I'm not going backwards.

In Daegu at the 2011 world championships when I hit it, the throw was perfect, for me, at that stage of my career. When I look back on last season, how we started, and how we progressed over the season, we were well ahead at the same time of the year in 2012.

Last year, in my first competition in Oslo, I threw 20.26 metres, and then progressed from there. But in 2012 we got one step ahead of that. JP has had it all planned out through to my last competition of the year. I know exactly what I'm doing every day, and I believe in everything he gives me to do.

It might surprise people to know we've never done a full video analysis. Jarrod Adams, an athlete from Dunedin, was present when I was throwing one day, and he videoed me on an iPhone. I had a quick look at it and so did Jean-Pierre. He said to me, 'I saw there is still much more there. Your hip is not quite finishing the work. You threw well, but there is still more there.'

Jean-Pierre feels the throw. That's why he stands at the back of the circle. It's great because if he looks at it, and feels it, and knows it's going to be a great throw, he says 'Yes' before I've even released the shot.

When he says that, he's always right. He has the eye for the event, the eye for the discipline. He lives and eats and breathes it, and he's done so for many years. He's moulded one great shot-putter in Werner Gunthor, and now he's redefining my career. I'm better technically now than I ever was.

A lot of people have commented on how much more dynamic and athletic I've become. Before I was big and strong and I smacked the crap out of it. I still smack the crap out of it, but I'm technically in a more stable position when I do that.

June: New York

Originally, we were going to compete in London in July as part of a two-day meeting, but the organisers said they were moving the women's shot put from London to Monaco.

We needed to do two comps in July, freshening up before the Olympics, and we wanted two before that, so, hard on the heels of Rome, I was off to New York, with only eight clear days between them.

You want to keep competition fitness inbuilt in you and not completely gone. We didn't want to waste the competition phase. There needs to be something to keep the spark going.

I went back to Magglingen for four days' training, and then I jumped on a plane in Zurich for an eight-hour flight to New York. This time Jean-Pierre didn't come with me. A little bit of jet lag hit me when I arrived; there's a six-hour time difference from Switzerland, which is a slightly bigger change than you might expect.

The New York Diamond League event was held in Icahn Stadium on Randall's Island, which is in the East River off Manhattan. We were staying on 42nd Street at the Grand Hyatt, which in theory is about 30 minutes away from the stadium. But this is New York traffic. Go at the wrong time and it becomes a big trip. A track was made available for athletes to practise on, but a friend who did that found it took 90 minutes to get there and 90 minutes to get back.

Usually, when we're staying at a hotel for the Diamond League they arrange for you to have all your meals at the hotel. But in New York you get instead a $US50 a day allowance for your three meals. In New York you're not going to be splashing out with $50, and you're sure not going to be out on the streets in your casual sports gear, which, of course, you can wear when you're getting room service in a hotel. You have to spend time finding good and simple food to eat.

It's quite distracting, and you don't really want to be eating out all the time. I love New York as a tourist, but what I'm doing is competing, trying to make sure I'm in the best shape possible. New York isn't a place where it's ever easy to sleep, or chill. It's a 24-hours-a-day city.

The city is buzzing, which is great if you're relaxing and enjoying it. I'd go back any day. But the competition itself was poorly run. There was very little information and so there were a lot of unhappy athletes. As far as getting to the comp, and being as little fatigued as possible, it was not a 10 out of 10 by any means.

I had to find my own gym, and eventually went to a public one. For the tonifying session I wasn't allowed to bring a friend onto the floor with me. They said they didn't allow other coaches onto the floor.

'We have a contract with our own trainers, so she can't be there.'

'But she's not coaching, she's just assisting. Are your trainers going to spot [assist] me?'

'Oh no, you'll have to pay for that.'

When I first arrived in New York I was still thinking, 'Okay, this is going to be good.' But by the morning of the competition, the way I felt, I had it in my head that I'd be happy if I was going to throw 20.50 metres. I was going to be happy with anything over that. You always have to take the positives from the negatives.

The stadium itself, which was built in 2005, is very small. The crowd wasn't large at all, and there was no real hype. The circle itself was terrible. There were actually small holes in it, and it wasn't quick.

My mum Lilika and dad Sidney's wedding feast in Tonga. It was an arranged marriage, and after the wedding Dad brought Mum back to New Zealand.

Mum was the angel of all angels, and her views were old school on how my sister Paddy (in blue) and I should behave.

After Mum and Dad spilt up, we moved with Mum to Tonga. I started primary school there.

Back in New Zealand, at my Dad's place, with Paddy, and my half-brother Sydney.

Above: Mangere East Primary
School, 1994. I'm the fairly tall girl
in the middle row in the white top.

Left: With my school friend
Victoria Filimoehala in 2001.
By then I'd been to two youth
world championships, in Poland
and Hungary — a big learning
curve for a kid from Mangere.

At my first world youth championships in Poland, 1998, a 14 year old from a fresh-off-the-boat background suddenly in a white kids' world. I finished 10th.

With Kirsten Hellier at my next world youth championships, in Debrecen in Hungary, in 2001. This time I won, and set a championship record.

With Erica Farrelly at Mum's grave. At primary school Erica stepped in and took a punch in the eye for me. She's been my best friend ever since.

The last photo I had with Dad before he died. It took time for us to forge a relationship, but at the end he was able to tell me he loved me.

Above: The world youth team in Hungary, 2001.

Right: My first tattoo, a tribute to Mum.

At the Manchester Commonwealth Games in 2002 I won silver. In the centre is the winner, Vivian Chukwuemeka, from Nigeria, and the bronze medallist is Johanna Abrahamse, from South Africa.

Happier times, in 2004, with Bertrand Vili, the year we got married.

The early days with Kirsten as my coach were exciting, and successful. Here I've just won the silver medal at the 2002 Commonwealth Games.

They had school kids running as part of the meeting. I'm all for kids' athletics, but there's a time and place. We had to sit there while they ran two 4 x 400-metres relays, out there for an hour before the competition with no shade at all, in 30°C heat and 90 per cent humidity. I was really tired: jet-lagged, hot and sweaty. I tried to get up, doing what I could.

My first throw was shit, 19.13 metres, but you've always got to keep your first throw. I managed to pop out 20.60, which was okay. I'd thrown what I predicted that morning, so I walked away as happy as I could be in the circumstances.

Basically, I threw like crap. My legs weren't working, and I was mentally and physically tired. But you have to try to do what you can. I still managed to win, and threw over 20 metres three times. By the time we'd finished I was a little dehydrated from the heat and light-headed, almost like minor heat stroke.

Afterwards I met up with Michelle Pickles and her TV3 cameraman. It was good to see a familiar face.

Jean-Pierre and I talked on the phone, and he was happy with what I threw, but he wanted to know what the weather was like, what the circumstances of the meeting were. He's good in that way.

The first bus back to the hotel wasn't for a couple of hours, so I got a taxi back to the city. That night I met a friend, and I didn't really want to walk around a lot, so we took one of those open-topped buses, doing a three-hour tour, looking round New York. We ended up in Times Square, and went to Bubba Gump's for dinner, which is a lot of fun, a happy, noisy place. It was a good ending to the night. By the time I got back to the hotel I was totally exhausted, just able to crawl into bed and get to sleep.

The next night at 6 pm I flew back to Switzerland. The last

bus to the airport was leaving at 1 pm, so there were a lot of hours spent at the airport, people watching. The travel and the heat caught up with me there. I felt light-headed, sleepy and a little nauseous. The flight was seven hours overnight, and then I caught the train from the airport home. All the way in the train I was doing that twitchy, head-bobbing thing where you start to slump forward asleep and then start awake.

I got to Biel, the city at the base of the mountain where Magglingen is, at 10.30 am, went to bed at 11, and told Sarah Cowley, who was in Magglingen working to qualify for the Olympics in the heptathlon, to come wake me at 2.30, otherwise I wouldn't be able to sleep that night. I was still totally deeply asleep when she started banging on my door.

You need those sleep patterns back as quickly as possible. I had a meal the first night, went to bed at about 10, and slept right through to the morning. Then I was straight back into training.

Late June: black hole in the road

At the end of June I seemed to have got into a really dark hole, one that I felt I couldn't dig myself out of. Everything seemed too hard and I was emotionally hurting, missing my family so much. For about seven days I really just went through the motions of training. It was tough to the stage where there were a couple of almost teary throwing sessions.

That time was five weeks out from the Olympics. Was it a reaction to the hype of the Games? I don't think it was. There were a number of elements involved. I think a big one was that I'd been away from New Zealand for so long I had an almost desperate urge to see my family.

I also came to realise I was trying to be all things to all the Kiwi athletes who had come to Magglingen working towards the Olympics. I love them dearly, but I started to stress over how they were progressing, what they needed help with, rather than looking after my own stuff. I was stressing over shit I shouldn't have been stressing over. There's no point trying to be a superhero, with a dozen things running through your mind.

There were strong conflicting feelings involved. As much as I loved people being here, it got to the stage where I felt that my personal space, my little mountain nest, was being invaded.

But after you've hit rock bottom there's only one way to go, and that's up. I clawed myself out of it with the help of the support team around me. From that time every week got better and better. The loving man Jean-Pierre is, he helped pull me out of this black hole, and get me heading forward.

A turning point, too, was when my chiropractor, Ed Timings, flew from Auckland right at the end of June, and spent a weekend helping me. I really needed him. I had golfer's elbow, and my back was really tight. He fixed me physically, with his chiropractic skills, but it was also great that he was there for me. When Ed came he provided me with a system to help me every day, a tool called the 'Circle of Life'.

Basically, I have a book in which I draw an inner circle, and in that circle is what I'm going to focus on today. Then, in the outer circle, what I'm not going to focus on. On 13 July, for example, in the inner circle I had myself and Jean-Pierre, because we were going to train, Lou Johnson, my physio, who joined me on 6 July, and — tah-dah — clothes washing.

The circumstances are such that it's what I have to do, and it's important I focus in this way. So every day I wake up and do it. On my outer circle I had my family, injuries, Lucerne (where I was going to compete on 17 July), the Olympics, Mike McGuigan, because he was coming over soon from Auckland, but I didn't need to focus on him yet, and my Games uniform. That item was there because I had received my uniform but it didn't fit. Let's not go into details, but the tights aren't comfortable to compete in. I mean, really, really not comfortable.

That's the sort of thing I have on the outside, so it's there, but I'm not going to dwell on it. So this was like my everyday bible for the Olympics, because I needed to stay focused, and not waste precious energy on bullshit, to put it bluntly. It really helped me a lot. During the bad period, every time I went to bed my mind would be whirling, thinking about the Games, about competing. Now it's great to do that, but there's a time and place, and just before going to bed is not the best time to do it.

Every time I thought about the Olympics I got goose bumps, I'd be really excited. But if you get like that too often you're wasting precious energy. You need to conserve it, so that when you train in the afternoon, let's say, you're ready to work like a trouper, to make sure you're in good health.

What I had on my mind was that I'd been in Magglingen for so long that I had to make sure what I did would work. I got my eye back totally set on the channel we trained for, and the journey that Jean-Pierre and I are on. It's been tough going, but I must say that JP has pulled me through a lot, believing in me and having confidence in what we're doing.

By the time I competed in Nancy in eastern France I felt powerful, I felt dynamic and I felt strong. And I felt happy, because I'd pulled myself up, and because I was in a good space, feeling positive again.

Jean-Pierre, Lou and I drove to Nancy, about a four to five-hour trip, on the morning before the competition, which was on Sunday, 8 July. A lot of the time I just lay in the back seat and slept while they drove and navigated.

The meet was part of the French national circuit, but quite a few international athletes came to it as well. In the shot put, though, it was only French girls.

It was an amazing circle and atmosphere in which to compete. In the shot they had a 20-metre line at the end of their border. Basically, they had fine gravel, then grass. At the 20-metre mark they had a concrete barrier. I asked them if they could put some sand down to cover the barrier in case it damaged my shot. They did, and because all my throws were over 20 metres, the last bit of every throw was slightly uphill. They would have measured a wee bit more if the ground had been flat. I threw 20.97 metres, but if it had been flat it would have been over 21 metres.

In some ways it would have been good to throw over that, but we decided that nobody else needed to know about it until after the Games. We just left it under the radar.

The throws were just popping off my hand. My goal in Nancy was to be consistent. If I threw over 21 metres, great, but that wasn't my goal; it was to throw from the word go with consistency. Bang, bang, bang, right there.

3
Embracing the love

I was born in Rotorua, on 6 October 1984. My older sister Patricia — Paddy — was a year old when I arrived.

My mum Lilika was the angel of angels. No sex before marriage, no alcohol, no smoking, no swearing, you name it. She was very religious, and had served her mission in the Mormon Church for two years before she married. I have to admit I would never be able to live up to her standards myself.

She was brought up by her grandparents in Tonga. Her uncle, who lived in Rotorua, thought she would have a better life in New Zealand and tried to get her over here. Her uncle was a good friend of my dad Sidney, and he got him to go to Tonga and meet my mum. It was an arranged marriage, held in Tonga, and then he brought her back to Rotorua.

Dad was 30 years older than my mother, who was only 21 when I was born, so Dad was 51 or 52. He was from Bristol in the English West Country, had been in the British Navy, and got off here in Opotiki. He told me once that when he arrived he went to prison for a month, but then he was able to get citizenship.

He was about 6 ft 8 in, a huge man. He had to get special shoes made for him; I still have a pair at home. He wasn't only tall; he was also big, very solid. There's tall and lanky, but in our family we're quite lucky, we're mainly tall and strong. That mix of the English side and the Island side is a good combination for us — very good genes, really.

Dad was a hard-working man; in fact all the Adams family are hard-working people. He was a logging driver, working 12, 13-hour shifts and doing that real manly stuff: building the house, cutting the wood, doing all the work at home.

My mother was a strong woman, and she was very strong with us. Mum was old school. If she said this is it, it was. No boyfriends, none of that. My older sister was the rebel, and Paddy and my mother would argue continually. But I never liked upsetting my mother. If she would come to give me a hiding I'd run and hide in a cupboard. Paddy would run out the door and not come back. I think I didn't want Mum to be more upset about it. I'd always say, 'Yes, Mum,' and if she was going to thrash me I'd put myself in a corner.

Mum and Dad split when I was about three. Mum, Paddy and I were living together. We stayed in Auckland a couple of years and then we went back to Tonga.

That's where my mother met her second husband, Tevita, who became my stepfather. We stayed in Tonga and went to primary school in a place called Fahefa for a couple of years.

We moved back to New Zealand when I was seven, and then Mum had my younger sister Ana in 1990. We were basically brought up by Mum and Tevita in the Tongan way, in the Tongan culture. Paddy and I always felt that Ana, being the baby of the family, was spoilt rotten. It seemed to us that she got everything. You know how older kids are. I actually love my little sister with all my heart.

Ana is the double of my mother. She's short and has darkish

skin. She once told her friends at school, 'Valerie's my sister.' And her friends said, 'No she's not. Stop lying man, you're bluffing, you're bluffing.' She told me, 'Can you come to school? I want to bum them out.' I turned up and it's like *bro'Town*. They're like, 'Oww, Ana, that's your sis-ta?'

We lived in Mt Roskill to start with, and then we moved into Tevita's brother's house in Mangere, and next we moved into our own place in Mangere.

My first year at school in New Zealand was at Owairaka Primary, and then to Mangere East Primary, Mangere Intermediate and finally Southern Cross Campus in Mangere East.

Tevita was basically our dad, because our father wasn't around. We were brought up quite strongly in the Mormon Church and were all baptised as Mormons. All five of us together as a family were sealed in the Temple, which in the Mormon faith basically means you're bonded with your family in the eyes of the church. As a family, it was a fantastic time really.

At primary school was when we got started in sports. I was head and shoulders taller than anyone else there, so I got all the nasty words: 'Bigfoot', 'Giant' and the rest.

I had one friend, Erica, who came to Mangere from a wee town up north, and she's still my best friend to this day. Red hair, skin so white that if she gets sunburnt she's like a lobster. She had no friends when she arrived, because she was new to the school, and I befriended her. We were even pen pals, although she lived just two streets up the road.

In standard four there was a big kid called Manu in the same class as Erica and me. One day his little sister was being a cow to me. So I told her to shove it, and she went and told Manu. He came up at lunchtime to punch me. Erica stood in front of me and said, 'Don't touch my friend.' He just belted her one, gave her a big black eye.

She was so tiny, and she took a punch for me. She had to go home to her mother and explain what had happened. Then the principal got involved and from that day Erica's always been my best friend.

The hardest years were at intermediate school. You hope to go there with your friends from school, and obviously there are a lot of other kids, and you're only there for two years.

I don't know if kids now find intermediate pretty tough. But for me it was the worst; I hated it. Lots of new kids, kids who are a little bit older, puberty, there are boys you like, then you have the pretty skinny girls, and the nerdy ones, the fat ones, and all those things start to matter.

I got in some trouble at intermediate, I swore at a teacher, but I was just so frustrated at times with being mocked. But one thing I never did when I was being teased was smash anyone.

There's one thing I did that I'm sort of proud of, but also not really. There's one person others can't tease me about and that's my mother. A boy turned round and said to me, 'Your mother's an effin' fat bitch.' You can call me what you like, and I might give you the fingers, but I won't touch you. But this guy should never have said that about my mother. I got up out of my chair, walked straight over and I punched him in the forehead. He had to have four stitches to close up the cut. I was angry. He's still got the scar on his forehead.

My sister Paddy's even worse. In primary school a guy called my mother names, and I told Paddy. She chased him round the whole school four times until she caught him, and scratched the hell out of his face. We got taken home to Mum, and she gave us a hiding. But the principle was: do not talk about my mother.

I was 13, in Year 10, when I took up throwing. At Southern Cross Campus it's a compulsory part of school athletics. I threw the shot at the school championships and broke the school record by a couple of metres. At the Counties-Manukau championships a couple of weeks later, I broke the record there by two metres. We turned up late, and I threw in bare feet.

I didn't really think too much about it. My first love was basketball. My sister and I were playing for Counties-Manukau rep teams, and for Auckland age-group teams. Track and field was there, but it was sort of something you had to do at the school.

Then we went to the North Island secondary schools athletics meet where I won. Next I went to my first secondary schools nationals in Massey Park in 1999. I was shitting myself. I came second to a girl called Monique Taito. I was pretty tall, but she was quite a big girl. That was pretty amazing, and I got a silver medal.

In 1998 I'd been training with a sprint coach, Russ Hoggard, at the Counties-Manukau club, and he introduced me to another coach, Kirsten Hellier. I'd been training with her maybe seven weeks before the nationals.

I think I didn't really know my potential until they told me I'd qualified for the world champs.

I was only 14 when I had my first trip overseas, to a place called Bydgoszcz in Poland. That was the first time they held a world youth championships, for athletes under 18, and I finished in tenth spot.

I was homesick like you wouldn't believe. I'm a homebody really. I called my mother collect every day on the calling card they used to have back in the day. I'd cry on the phone all the time. But it was also the best experience for me. Mum was pretty proud that I did it after just six months of training.

The team was managed by Brett Addison, and Wendy

Brown, the former sprint champion, a very awesome lady, was my first team coach. Before we left she came to training to pick up some tips, things that Kirsten would want me to work on.

I'd never left New Zealand other than to go to Tonga, and I was going from Mangere to Poland. It wasn't like the three-hour plane ride to the Islands; it took about 40 hours to get there.

Getting the money together for the trip was a haul as well. I was lucky enough to have had a guy called Peter Sykes from the great Mangere East Family Service Centre helping out, and he did a lot of fundraising for me.

Mum and Dad were really poor. My stepfather wasn't very well, so he could do only casual labouring work. They couldn't really give me $20 to tide me over and still be able to run the household properly. But Peter was able to raise enough to pay my fares over there, and get me pocket money and my uniform.

It was pretty scary. One thing I do remember is that my uniform didn't really fit me properly. It's a problem that seems to have gone on through the years.

Staying together with the team, where I think I was one of the youngest, was all very new to me. It was a massive learning curve.

There were two throwers, Victoria Lowrie and me. She was a North Shore Bays girl. The people in the team were all white, whereas I come from a fresh off the boat background, and people do things differently.

What they pack is different. For me to take on the plane my Mum had bought me Biguns chips and a big budget-brand fizzy drink. When I got all that I thought I was the most spoilt kid in the world. When we hopped on the plane, all the white kids had their little snacks that Mum and Dad had bought for them, the nice Cadbury chocolates and little Tim Tams, which are a bit more expensive than what my Mum could buy. Different living.

We went to England first and competed in some meets there. That was great. At the championships in Poland it really was a whole new world to me. There were even little local kids who wanted autographs. You're signing autographs at the age of 14.

There were, of course, athletes from all over the world. One American girl gave me a badge and said she was from Nebraska. I had no idea then where it was. Tonga, Samoa, yes. Nebraska was a mystery to me.

The whole experience made me a lot hungrier to find out what it might be like at a higher level. It gave me a lot of motivation to continue, a taste of what might be possible.

When I came back from Europe, Mum put on a big feast for me at the park next to our home. Peter Sykes got some tents organised and some chairs, and Mum had re-ribboned all my medals. It was just before Christmas. She was really proud.

Kids are cruel, but things got easier as my track and field career began. I never went to a school ball. I was just too big, couldn't find shoes to fit, couldn't afford good clothes to wear. Paddy was skinnier, prettier, and all the boys liked her. The boys all chased her. She was beautiful and I was the tomboy.

But on the sportsfield, playing basketball and doing track and field, I felt like I fitted in. I got confident, and I was able to put my size into use.

It was really happy times until Mum got sick. I was only 14 when she started getting sick, and I'd just started athletics at that stage.

After the world champs Kirsten continued to coach me. I was part of Counties-Manukau, and we worked together three times a week, then up to six days a week as it got more serious.

I stayed at school, and turned 15 in 2000. My stepfather Tevita wanted to go to America to get some work to help out the family financially, so he went over there. By then Paddy had left, with just Ana and me at home. I'd go to work at Pizza Hut, waitressing, and I got my driver's licence.

In 1998 Mum had a hysterectomy because cancer had been found. Two years later she had to go back for a test, and it had spread very rapidly. She went from a normal consultation at the hospital to being in bed and drugged up with morphine.

My mum's aunty came to my house and looked after my little sister. At the hospital in 2000 it was just me and Mum in July and August. It was a pretty tough time. Mum didn't trust the nurses to do things for her, so I had to care for her. She didn't want them to take her for a shower, to lift her. She felt comfortable that I could lift her. She was quite a big lady, but I was quite a big girl, so I'd bathe her, feed her, take her for a walk, do whatever she wanted.

During the last couple of weeks she was getting sicker, and then I got pneumonia. I was sleeping on the tiles next to her bed, and they'd given me a sheet to put on the ground, but it wasn't very comfortable. I'd tend to Mum during the night, so I wasn't sleeping well.

The staff weren't particularly nice to us during that time. I think they thought I was older than what I was, so they didn't really help out a lot.

Then at the end of August, early September, Mum got worse quite quickly and they said we were moving to a hospice. They hadn't been able to do anything for her other than give her pain relief. I wasn't told directly that there was nothing more they could do; it was more implied.

When they moved us out I just thought we'd overstayed our

time at the hospital. My assumption at the time was that we'd been moved out because they needed the bed.

We got put in an ambulance and moved to a hospice near Totara Park and were placed in a room. It was like going into a house. It didn't smell like a hospital, didn't feel like a hospital. It felt like home, and I thought, 'Ah, sweet.' I didn't become aware of what a hospice was until later on.

Mum was still aware of what was going on, able to speak to us, and we got settled in. While we were staying there we called our stepfather to come back from America, and a week later he arrived.

The week before I'd push her round in the bed, because she couldn't really walk, and then I'd carry her to the shower. Get her some food. It was really nice. It was a big room, and I had my own bed, our own bathroom and a La-Z-Boy chair. I thought, 'Oh my God, this is awesome.'

Little did I know there was a two-week limit to a stay at the hospice. Usually, by the time two weeks comes around things happen.

One night I was trying to get Mum from A to B, and she fell. I couldn't lift her up, because she was in an awkward position. So the nice hospice people called six fire-fighters to come in and these guys arrived and helped us lift Mum up onto the bed. I thought it was really neat that they were able to call on these people to come and help us out.

That was the first week, and she was good, just a little bit sleepy here and there. The second week came and Tevita turned up. At this time a lot of people were visiting, and Mum was so doped up on morphine she'd drift in and out of consciousness.

One day I remember Kirsten turned up with her son Jarod, her youngest boy, who was only a baby then, and Mum would hold him and then she'd slump and I'd have to hold him. Then she'd wake up and say, 'What are you doing?'

'You're dropping the baby,' I'd say.

'No I'm not.' She'd hold him again then all of a sudden, drop. We'd have a little battle.

When Tevita came Mum had the best week ever. I thought, 'Great, we're getting better now. Wow, all you needed was the fix of seeing your husband.'

Come the night of 15 September I was watching the opening ceremony of the Sydney Olympics. It was fairly early, but Tevita and Mum were asleep, Ana was sleeping on a mattress on the floor, and I was in the La-Z-Boy watching the ceremony. I was thinking, 'This is so awesome, I so want to be there. Mum's getting better. This is all sweet.'

I fell asleep, and I was woken up quite early, five o'clock in the morning, by Mum. She wasn't feeling good, and everything had deteriorated. I took her to the bathroom, then I had to wake everybody up. By 8 am they'd called the doctors, and when they checked Mum I asked what was happening. The doctor just sort of closed his eyes and nodded, indicating, 'This is it.'

I was trying to keep it together, crying my eyes out at the same time. Tevita knew what was happening. Ana was just 10, but she didn't really know.

I then called Paddy to come, and then Mum's aunty, Mafi, to come. She turned up.

By now it was about quarter to nine, and we were all in the room. Mum did something really interesting. She sat up on the bed, and she called my little sister. She kissed her and hugged her and told her to move over. She told Tevita to sit in front of her and hold her hand, and then she told me to come and sit next to her. I couldn't hold back my tears, and she looked at me and breathed slowly, and rested her head on me.

Then she looked outside, through the window she was facing, and then her breathing got slower and slower. In the Tongan tradition, Matafonua, you take a last sighting of the earth you were brought up in.

Then she slept, and was gone. Her weight fell against me, and I was holding her like a baby. I told my young sister, 'She's gone.' Ana fell to the ground, and banged her head on the floor with her pain.

I was crying quite quietly, but really painfully, trying to hold her. Then I lay her down properly on the bed.

It was amazing how she had set it up, how she positioned everyone where she wanted them. She knew what was happening.

We kept living with my stepdad. I didn't go back to school for several weeks. Tongan funerals don't take one day, and I couldn't face going back. At the end of that year I basically went to school just to eat my lunch.

At the funeral my Mum's first cousin Henry Kata led the service, and then in January he passed away. In February, unbeknown to me, Tevita was dating his wife.

That month I went over to New Caledonia for a throwing meet. When I went away the house was how Mum had left it. While I was away Tevita and Henry's widow got married, and when I came back all my mum's stuff was in one room. That was the start of the end of it for me and Tevita.

Until then we'd got on really well. I was hoping to be able to get on with my sport, and give him back some of the help he'd given to me. He'd been kind and good to my mother, and her life was him.

When I came back it was a completely different story. I think he was a bit lost without my mother. She was the rock of the family.

I had to find somewhere to live, and in May I went and stayed with an aunt in Hillsborough for a few months. At this stage I'd qualified to go again to a world youth champs, this time in Hungary in 2001. Kirsten was the coach.

In that year I caught up with my father again. I went back to Rotorua to visit. At first I was quite standoffish. He'd remarried, and they had four kids, so it was pretty odd for me, but I was happy to reconcile with him. My attitude was that he is my parent, and he's the only parent I've got left. The next six years were the best years ever with him, realising he went through a fair bit of shit himself, but at the end, before he passed away, he was able to tell me that he loved me.

As a person he was very stubborn, very much the Englishman. He still had a West Country accent after being in New Zealand for 60 years.

We kept in regular touch. When I could I'd go down there and see him. He had stomach cancer and had emphysema as well. He'd smoked for years, and giving it up for the last three years of his life was too late.

In 2007 while I was going down to see him every weekend, I had to go to Shizuoka in Japan for a competition. He wasn't so good when I went away. He'd lost 20 kilos in one month. He couldn't hold food. I was really sad to go. He told my sister Viv that if something happened not to tell me. I competed in Shizuoka but that went like shit.

We stopped in Sydney on the way home, and I turned my phone on and got a text saying, 'As soon as you get home go to Rotorua, Dad's not well.' The two hours on the plane from Sydney was the longest time of my life.

I arrived home that afternoon, went straight to Rotorua, and everybody was there, everyone in New Zealand, and a brother who'd come from Rarotonga. Dad had stopped talking. He was breathing, but he wasn't able to respond in words. I went up to see him at about 8.30 pm, told him I was there. I was the last person to arrive. He passed on at about 10.30. So I was fortunate to be there for both my mum and my dad.

Two weekends before, we'd watched *The Godfather*. Part one the first weekend, part two the second. He was a *Godfather* fanatic. He knew every character, what they were up to. The sad thing was that before I went to Japan he had said, 'We'll watch part three when you get back.'

In 2005 I organised a reunion for Dad and I managed to get 13 people there. Just for the sake of 'We might all grow up and not know we're going out with our cousin.' I knew there were other brothers and sisters. Along the way we'd found out about the basketball players Warren and Ralph Adams. Ralph used to pop in and see us when I was with Mum and my stepfather.

Rob Tualave took his mother's surname. Rob didn't know that Warren and Ralph were his brothers, although people said to him he looked like them.

There are 17 of us brothers and sisters counted, with 21 suspected. We have a Maori mother, we have a Pakeha, we have two Tongans, we have another half Maori, half white, and a Tokelauan.

We joke among ourselves, saying we have them in lots. A lot of four, then a stress release, then another stress release, a lot of two, then a stress release, then a lot of two, then a stress release — just mocking my father doing that.

When we're all together we get on like a house on fire. The Adams kids are mostly tall, with maybe three not so tall. I'm the tallest female, and the youngest one, Steven, is the tallest male. He's like 7 ft.

I'm pretty close to some of my brothers. The culture has a big influence on how you're brought up, and how you regard family. My mother brought up me and Paddy, and Rob's mother brought him up. The last lot my Dad mainly brought up and there are others he had a big influence on.

The culture and the respect, the way the Tongans do it, embracing people, is quite different to the way other races may do it.

4

The best feeling ever

Eighty thousand people are in the Beijing Olympic stadium they call the Bird's Nest as I step into the circle for my first throw.

It's the final of the women's shot put at the 2008 Games. My aim is simple. Smash the first throw. Just smack the crap out of it, then let the other girls chase it if they can.

I'm aware there's a huge number of people here, and I love competing in front of a big crowd. Here in New Zealand at nationals there are perhaps a couple of hundred people. Or at a normal track meet maybe there are just two, so going somewhere where there's a lot of people really pumps you up.

Later in the same night Usain Bolt is going to run his 100 metres final. You can imagine how everybody was screaming their heads off. You're dealing with the hype of it all. I'm aware of the people being there, but my focus is on concentrating on one thing, what I'm here for.

I can hear everybody, and it's an amazing atmosphere, but I don't let myself relax and take it all in. That'd be a distraction. Some people can perform under that pressure, and some can't. At the end of the day you're there to compete, but it's a show for a lot of people. They're there to watch you try to beat someone who's trying to beat you back.

When they announce your name over the big speaker, there's a roar from the stands. You want to use that to your advantage. Some athletes can't deal with that. I'm quite lucky that at a very young age I found I was okay with it.

Adrenalin lifts me up. They call my name, and I step into the circle. I start to move and I feel like I'm flying across the circle. The throw is easy, and when it feels easy it goes a long way. If it feels hard, and you've struggled, and you're trying too hard then it's a crap throw. You know that from experience, from past performances.

When the distance comes up it's 20.56 metres, a personal best. Of course I'm pleased, but at this level you don't let your guard down for a second. There are five rounds to go, five rounds to realise a dream.

I'd arrived in Beijing just three days before the qualifying rounds. The lead-in hadn't been great. I went to Townsville for two weeks and then to Brisbane for a week. I went to Townsville because it was a bit hotter than normal, and in Beijing in August the temperatures get up to around 30°C.

We went to Australia for the heat mainly, and it was closer to home than going early to China. We had a friend called Yvonne Mullins who's the executive director of the Oceania Athletic Association and she hooked us up there. They had training facilities there that I'd used, and competed at, although not for that long or before an Olympics.

It looked ideal, but when I was in Townsville I had an allergic reaction to the pH of the water. If the pH of a swimming pool is too high or too low your skin burns and itches. That's what happened to me from showering.

I had to get iced down at night to go to sleep. It was really bizarre. The doctor said I was allergic to the water, so I had to bathe in Pinetarsol and slap on sun lotion. That wasn't fun. I panicked a little bit because I really wasn't very good. I'd be in a shopping mall and it'd be so itchy I was scratching my back against a counter. It was horrible. Then I had a week in Brisbane and the allergy started to calm down.

In Brisbane they have the Institute of Sport, which was perfect. Everything was at our feet really; we had no problems with training venues and times. It is an English-speaking country, and you know what you are eating. There are all those small things that you wouldn't be so sure of if you went to an unknown place.

You're tapering down at that stage. You keep up the quality but you're not doing as much work. Before then I was training twice a day, six days a week. Next, it went down to maybe once a day for three days, and then once a day for a couple of days.

It's a lot of short, sharp sessions, keeping the weights quite high, sort of a feel-good session, feeling powerful and strong and fast and dynamic. But not killing yourself so you become tired. All the tapering continued on while we were in Beijing right up to the day before competition. I was in the gym and out throwing, and doing lots of sprints. You do it on your own, not with a group of other athletes.

With me in Brisbane were my coach Kirsten Hellier and Lou Johnson my physio, who came over just for the last week to do some adjusting.

For me the 10 days before a major event are the days where it's crucial that you don't hurt yourself. I wear running shoes when I walk out of the house. Just being very careful what you do: no silly things, which I like to so sometimes. Stupid things, like climbing up a big fence and jumping off it. You cut that stuff out. You basically wrap yourself up in cotton wool because anything could happen.

I am a quite private person, and I do spend most of my time with the people I know. The New Zealand javelin champion, Stuart Farquhar, and his coach, Debbie Strange, came out during that time. I always have my sister on hand to talk to, but apart from that I keep everything pretty tight. During that time I don't like to talk to the media because there's no point in putting yourself in a position where you're under pressure. You try not to think about the competition, but it's very hard not to, because it's the biggest competition of your life.

While I was in Australia I was bumped down from second to third in the world rankings. One of the Belarusians, Natallia Mikhnevich, did a competition in Europe and threw 20.70 metres, so I was ranked number three going into the Olympics, behind another Belarusian, Nadzeya Ostapchuk, who had thrown 20.86 metres, and Mikhnevich. My personal best at that stage was 20.54 metres.

You think about the competition, you think about what's going to happen when you get there, the team environment, what the whole thing is going to be like.

I knew that the hype would be crazy, and that I needed to stay calm and focused on what I needed to do. I'd been to Beijing in May when they had a dummy run for the Games. That competition didn't go so smoothly. I did win, but none of the top-ranked throwers were there. Whether or not we'd gone there didn't really matter to me. I just didn't want any distractions.

For me the biggest distractions came from the New Zealand Olympic Committee — the NZOC — and management. It's pretty sad, but when I went to the Olympics in 2004 I didn't feel that they gave a shit about me.

I'd finished eighth after having appendicitis and surgery just six weeks before the Games. I didn't think finishing eighth at my first Olympics was a big disgrace. But it was in their eyes. Straight after I competed they couldn't give me the time of day. I don't forget people who dump on you.

We flew straight from Brisbane to Beijing. I arrived quite late, wanting just to get in, have a shower and go to bed. But there were about eight people at the airport to pick me up.

Out there, rolling out the red carpet, are the NZOC. I think, 'You guys didn't give a shit about me four years ago, so why now? Is it because my status has gone up, I've won world championships, there's a chance I can get a medal?' I knew why they did it. I'm quite real. They asked if they could take my bags. I said, 'No, that's fine. I can look after my bags, thank you very much.'

So I went into the village quite late. Got the keys, had dinner, had a massage, went to bed.

There were three days before I competed, and I was asked to talk to the media, but I turned down the requests. I wasn't going to jeopardise my chances of winning. I felt my only obligation was to get over the jet lag, get myself ready to compete, and go out and do the job. There's really nothing you can say to a journalist. If you say you're going to do really well, it can come back and bite you in the butt.

I'm a one-liner. I've never walked in saying I'm going to win. I've always said, 'My aim is to defend my title' or 'I'm going to try my best. I really want to win that medal for my country.'

I've learned with media people that you're going to love some of them and you're going to hate some. I've worked out who I can trust and who I can't. I think it's a bit different if you're in a team; if your team fails they're not going to come and attack you. In my situation, because it's an individual sport, if I fail, I'm going to be hounded the next day.

When I've finished competing, yes, there are obligations left, right and centre, to go to the media centre, to go to functions the officials have organised.

I felt good in Beijing. But I was nervous, too, and that's good. If you're not nervous you get a bit complacent.

When you get into the village you see thousands of people, and then by odd chance you might see Nadzeya Ostapchuk, or the German or the American thrower. There's a training venue where everybody in track and field goes, so you see them there on occasion, or perhaps at the gym when you're lifting.

Of course you try to put on your game face and start lifting your big weights, all that sort of shenanigans. I didn't actually throw at all while I was there. But I did a lot of warm-up routines, sprinting, loosening up the body. I had only three days of training before I competed.

Basically, it's funny, because the war of nerves starts from the word go. Before the competition you hardly talk to each other. You keep the other athletes at bay, so to speak, then when it finishes, you see them, have a talk and have a drink together.

I was nervous because, first of all, it was the biggest competition of my life. Also, there was a lot of expectation from people at home, much more than in 2004. This time I'd won a world championship, in 2007, so I guess some thought, 'Sweet, that's one gold in the bag.'

But I always knew that Nadzeya Ostapchuk and Natallia Mikhnevich had thrown further than me. On paper I didn't have a chance in hell, but my theory is that in competition what's on paper doesn't mean jack. It's a clean slate. Whether you're ranked first or eighth, anything can happen.

They had two groups in qualifying on the Saturday morning, 17 August. To make the final you needed to throw 18.75 metres. I threw 19.73 metres with my first throw, and that was all I was going to do. I packed up and went back to the village, ASAP.

Saturday night. It wouldn't have mattered where I was positioned in the order, but I'm number four, which works in my favour. To have the rest of the girls chasing me was my tactic from the first go.

My first throw is good, a big one, but I don't let my guard drop. I count down every throw, as if you're shooting ducks. First round gone, second round gone, third round gone. And every round Ostapchuk is coming up slowly, and then Mikhnevich passes her, with 20.28 metres, and starts making progress.

You can see my attitude on my face — don't even bother trying to make friends with me during that time. It's do or die for me. It has to be that way. The whole competition my nerves are so high, but somehow I contain them. I get this serious 'don't eff with me' look, and that's when I'm in my zone, and my game face is on.

In the whole competition I hardly sit down. I walk around, and sometimes I sneak a look at the board to see what the others are throwing. I never let my guard down.

I see Nadzeya Ostapchuk stressing out. She's on the bench doing press-ups, she's jumping around trying to get herself going, but there's nothing happening for her. By the fifth round she's broken through from sitting fifth to third, and then Natallia Mikhnevich has her final throw. I'm the last thrower. The last round is the best because I'm counting them off. It's 'Okay, you're gone, no more. I'm still first.' Then Ostapchuk throws, and she's gone. The last one is Mikhnevich.

It's a big throw, but I don't know how far. You can't really see, and you don't want to get too excited if it isn't going to go your way. I have my shirt sort of half on, half off, thinking, 'Shit, if she's taken me I'll jump in there, but if she hasn't I'm not even going to throw.'

When I know I've won, there is a wave of emotions: happiness, relief, the lot. I signal to the Chinese officials that I've finished. I draw my hand across my throat, and it takes them a while to realise what I mean.

I high-five the competitors who want to with me, and then I'm running to the stand, across the track and Kirsten is making her way down. Natallia Mikhnevich, who got silver, had her husband Andrei watching in the stands. He gives me a handshake, and says congratulations.

Kirsten comes down, and I just yank her over the barrier. We're celebrating and I'm in complete shock. I have a thousand feelings running through my head. I almost hyperventilate because I'm so happy — and so relieved at the same time.

We're so happy because it's like job well done, 10 years from when it all started. You can't contain it. You start jumping round like a hooligan, start waving flags, and a Chinese official is trying to hold me back, pulling on my arm. I quietly pull my arm away, just look at her, and say, 'Don't fucking touch me.' I say to her, 'I've just won the Olympics. Come on, just let me go.' She's saying, 'Hurry up, we must go.' I give her the look and we just keep jumping around and celebrating.

The photographers come round and take lots of photos. It's really awesome.

When I went to Kirsten and hugged her, a couple of Kiwis threw a New Zealand flag down. I wrapped myself in it, so

I was New Zealand from top to toe. Before I'd left home I'd decided to go Kiwi with my hair, so I had half of it dyed white.

I go round the whole stadium to the media mixed zone with the flag, my bag and with a towel round my neck. I'm looking for my sister Vivian and my niece Amco. A cameraman is in front of me and he doesn't keep walking, and I'm not looking at him at all. I'm yelling out to people. Next thing I run into him and we both fall over. In the middle of my excitement, I grab my bag and carry on.

Then I see my Vivian and Amco, and that's great. Everybody is crying. Then we have to stop because Usain Bolt is running his 100 metres final. So we all have to be silent. He wins and breaks the world record, and then we're off again.

We go to the media mixed zone which feels like it takes forever. It's quite full on, but really cool.

Next we go to the press conference under the stand, and then it's time for a drug test. That does take me forever. I'm so excited, and so keen to get it done, but it takes me almost two hours. I just can't go. They give me water, they give me Powerade, I'm drinking so much it's coming out of my ears, but not from where it should. I'm so frustrated because I wanted to get away and celebrate.

When I complete the test I'm so happy, maybe more relieved at first, for myself and my family, and my country. If it had gone another way I was worried how people at home would have reacted. Even though I was ranked number three, if I came through with a silver, I worried some people would have been upset because nothing other than a win would have been accepted. I do feel that about some Kiwis in New Zealand. It's such a small country and we do so well. But we are very tough on our sportspeople.

The final was at 9 pm. So by the time I'd talked to the media, and done my drug testing, it was late. They didn't have the medal ceremony until the next day, Sunday, because it was so late.

That was fine because there was more time to celebrate. The previous day, the super Saturday, the Evers-Swindell sisters had won gold in the women's double sculls, and they'd already got their medals. I saw them on the Sunday and there was a lot of media to do, and then I went to see the sponsors, Visa and adidas, before the evening ceremony.

When we got back to the village I went to the dining hall and had something to eat with the people I was with. Then we were wandering very quietly back, because it was two in the morning. I kid you not, I walked around the corner, and there was the whole management doing the haka. I was standing there feeling, 'Oh my God, are you kidding me? Dig me a hole right now.'

I was so embarrassed to be a Kiwi right there. I felt, 'How dare you be so arrogant to do the haka now, when James Dolphin, my team-mate, is due to run the biggest race of his life, the 200 metres qualifier, at nine o'clock this morning.'

James was woken up by the noise and he was so shitty. I went and apologised to him, told him I was so sorry, it was never my idea, I had no idea they were going to do it. He was angry about being woken up, and he didn't run very well. He got bagged in the media the next day, and I could only think, 'What the hell is wrong with you guys in management?'

They'd already done it at the stadium. So why would they need to do it again?

The Canadian and South African teams were next door to us, and it wasn't as if it had been done quietly. Everybody was affected. It was so loud it echoed right through the apartment blocks. It was really sad to me.

The South Africans reached a point where every time our team did the haka they used their vuvuzelas, the really noisy horns they had at the football world cup, to try to drown it out. How embarrassing is that? Their chef de mission complained about the haka. I don't blame him.

I'd seen it in 2004, when Dave Currie was also the chef de mission. I felt like saying, 'Look, I really admire our culture, I admire and appreciate the Maori culture, but we're not all Maori. We respect it, but don't try to ram it down our throats.' In the Commonwealth Games team especially there's a lot of Pacific Islanders.

I was born in New Zealand, and I'm proud of that fact. I love my country, and I love representing it. But I'm actually Tongan, not Maori. There's a big difference.

Earlier in the evening leading into the presentation was the whole nine yards — get ready, get your best gear on and go to the track to get your medal. It was the most amazing feeling. I never thought I would cry, but it was an uncontrollable emotion.

You hear the national anthem, and everything that's happened in the last 12 months, even the last 10 years, all plays through your head, and then you enjoy the moment.

I cried so much it was kind of embarrassing. But it was the best feeling ever. Receiving your medal and hearing the anthem, you know you've really done it.

5

Breaking up

When Kirsten Hellier told me she didn't see how she could continue to coach me I was devastated.

We were alone in a room at Waipuna Hotel in Auckland on a Thursday afternoon in late March, 2010. The national championships were in Christchurch that weekend.

'I think I can't give you anything more to improve on,' Kirsten said. 'Things are not working out like they used to, and we're both different people now.' So she was going to pull out of coaching me. She was upset, I was upset. I didn't say much at all, just sat there a bit shocked and also sad. I'll always be so grateful and thankful for what she's done for me. Kirsten and I started working together when I was 13 years old. Over the next 12 years we trained six days out of seven together, travelled the world and won Olympic, world and Commonwealth titles. I babysat her little boy Jarod, even lived for a year as a teenager with her and her family.

How had it come to this? Let me tell you the full story, which may be different from what you've been led to believe.

I was a very tall 13 year old, who had won an all-Auckland schools shot put title, breaking the record, while throwing in bare feet.

Russ Hoggard, a sprint coach, let me train with some of his group, but he knew I needed advice from someone who actually worked on throwing. One late afternoon at Massey Park in Papakura he introduced me to Kirsten. At that time I wanted to look shorter than I was, so I kept my head down while we spoke. Russ was the one who asked if she'd take me on. Kirsten must have seen something there, because several years later she told me she went home that night and said to her husband Pat, 'I've just met a girl who will become an Olympic champion.'

My family was living in Mangere then, so during my time at the Counties-Manukau club I'd catch the train to Papakura and Kirsten would take me back home because it was too dark for me to return on the train. My mother really trusted her to not only train me but to pick me up and drop me off at quite a young age.

When Mum died Kirsten and Pat's house was like a second home to me. They took me, a teenager, in and really looked after me.

In 2001 I lived fulltime with them for 12 months. They had a little girl, Mikaela, and when their son Jarrod came along I helped them look after him. He was like my little boy. I was Aunty Val, and it was really nice.

I was reliant on Kirsten when Mum died. I had no parent figure and Kirsten filled that role, and her mother did, too. I had no one really, and they were there for me. That was the great part, the best part, of the relationship. Training together and living together worked when I was younger.

In athletics we grew and learned together. Kirsten was a javelin thrower, a former national champion, who knew the basics of shot put, but didn't know the real detail. While I was learning to throw the shot, she was learning to become a better coach at the shot. We tried this, tried that, tried new and different methods until we found what worked. In a way I was a guinea pig. Eventually, we found something that worked for a little while, and while it lasted we kept it. Then we tried other things, in an attempt to progress my technique as much as possible. It was a big learning curve.

We talked with other coaches. Jean-Pierre Egger, my present coach, was in New Zealand in 2001, and we did a couple of sessions with him, which was really awesome, because I knew his background, how he'd coached world champions, and how successful he'd been. As a 16 year old it takes your breath away. He had such mana, such an aura, and he was such a nice guy.

My feeling was that I was as strong as an ox, and my technique was okay, but I was never as confident with my technique as I am now. What gave me confidence was knowing I was strong enough to smash the crap out of it if I had to in order to get through.

It was fantastic when we were doing well, and breaking records and winning.

As a kid you don't question what a coach is doing. The added element was that I was brought up in the Tongan culture to respect your elders, so I went along with anything Kirsten wanted me to do. Eventually, though, you grow up, and the relationship starts to be a little different.

Looking back, when I met my husband, Bertrand Vili, things started to change. We got married in 2004 at St Mark's Church in Pakuranga. We didn't have a lot of money to do much, and my sister Paddy felt left out of the wedding, which was sad for me.

But the problems really started in 2006 when I went to have surgery for my shoulder. I was away in Germany and I can remember quite clearly that I was doing bench presses and it just tweaked. I always had problems with my long head bicep on the right-hand side, and I had to go back and do some reps on the bench.

That was the start of the bigger issues, from there. I came home and had surgery. While I was recovering I was trying to throw, to get back into it in time for the nationals. I threw 18 metres-something there, and then it was time for the world champs in 2007.

When we were preparing in Cairns, I threw really well in the first comp, and then in the second, at the Oceania champs, I screwed something up in my throwing hand, my finger. When I released the shot I felt a shooting pain. 'Oh shit.'

Soon as it was sore, Kirsten said, 'I think we should go home.' By this stage I had my strength back up to the way it was before the surgery. I felt I was okay. As we were just leaving the track she was already saying, 'We should go home,' and I was thinking, 'What the fuck man? Are you serious?'

I was crying because it was sore, and I was crying because I felt my career was on the line, and the world championships were just a week away. I was feeling like crap.

Kirsten was doing the silent treatment, which she was very good at. I don't handle that very well. When you're trying to compete, what you want is for your coach to be positive, to project the feeling they're supporting you. I had to be on my game all the time and try to compete well. When I didn't go well I could see she was unhappy. It was hard as hell.

So I was feeling terrible, because I was the one wanting to compete. I didn't know what to do.

Luckily, the team physio was there and really helped me through. I said, 'What can we do? What can we do?'

We had scans and tests, and I ended up having a cortisone shot in the torn ligament in my right-hand ring finger, the most vicious, painful experience of my life. They injected it the day before we went to Osaka. When we got there I didn't throw, but I did weights every day. I was constantly icing my hand. When I was lifting, squatting, cleans, snatches, it was fine, but when I went to bench it hurt a little bit. I put up with the pain, because I didn't want to rock the boat.

Kirsten wanted to have a test throwing session three days before I was due to compete to see what it was like. As you can imagine it was painful — eye-wateringly painful. I threw and I made 17 metres. I tried to throw as hard as I could. Kirsten didn't look very happy, but I was trying. She was just nodding, but no words were coming out of her mouth.

I was feeling like shit. The biggest competition of my life to that point was around the corner, and I was ranked No. 3, so I was a medal hope.

After I threw, the medical staff and management iced me up, which was really good. It was great to have them there, someone to talk to. I was feeling as bad as they were about the injury, and how it could affect me in competition.

The next day I lifted well, so Kirsten was back to being her normal self again, and then we went and competed.

As painful as my effing hand was I really tried my hardest to throw. I threw every round, sitting in second place. I think my pain threshold is pretty high, so I just dealt with it.

Every time I threw I went and stood next to the ice bucket. Nobody else knew I was injured, or picked up that I was. I opened the drinks container and I stood with my hand in there for the whole round, to numb the crap out of it. Get up, throw, back to the ice. Over and over.

So I got through the whole competition. I was behind Nadzeya Ostapchuk going into the last round. My best throw had been 19.95 metres. When it came to that last round I was nervous, but I was determined to do it. I threw 20.54 metres to win, and told the journalists, 'See that last put, that was for my dad.'

Of course, after I won Kirsten was a different person. I was happy that I'd won, I was happy that she was happy. She's the greatest when we're doing well and things are going well, but not so good when things are not going so well.

So I won throwing with a recovering torn ligament in my throwing hand. Also I was as big as a house, carrying the most body weight I ever have, which went on after my shoulder surgery. I wasn't able to be as active as I usually was, so I wasn't as athletic as I would have liked.

What I still had was strength. It was strength, rather than being dynamic, that got me through. I'm so much more athletic now than I was then.

We've won. Happy, happy, joy, joy. Let's have a party, it was great.

We went back to Germany to compete in the world finals, and Kirsten left to come home. I went to stay with my Aunty Valerie in Italy for a couple of days, then I came home, rested for a while, and started my Olympic build-up.

I started the Olympic campaign training pretty hard from the go. Then I went to the world indoors in Valencia and won. I came home and the real preparations started.

When we came back after the world indoors I thought, I'll try to drop a little bit of weight for the Olympics. My hand was fine by then, preparations went fine. My physio Lou was doing a lot of therapy for it; she was right onto it.

By this time Bertrand and I were having pretty serious problems. It wasn't a good situation when things went bad, because we were both being coached by Kirsten. If Kirsten was mad with Bertrand, or Bertrand was mad at Kirsten, I was piggy in the middle, as you can imagine. The blame for that situation didn't lie with Kirsten, because when Bertrand was being a real dick, I was trying to keep it from people I was training with.

Most of the time Bertrand and I trained together. It was often tense. I was trying to keep the peace with him, then with her, and then I had to go home with him.

So 2008 was the year from hell. For about three months every night Bertrand drank, coming home at three o'clock in the morning. I stayed awake waiting for him, scared he was going to get killed in a car accident.

Finally, in June I told him, 'You have to leave.' I bought him a ticket and told him to go. He had no remorse, no respect for what I wanted to do. I sent him off and I had one month before we went to Townsville.

Regardless of what was happening at my house, I was still able to go to training. Whether I was fighting with Bertrand or not, I'd still turn up to training. I was also trying my hardest to be a good wife, but at the same time I didn't want my Olympic dream to go down the drain because of him.

With very little time to go I had to bear down and focus on the Olympics.

When we went to Townsville to train before the Olympics and I had my skin problem it was difficult at times between Kirsten and me. A pattern emerged where everything would go very well, and then we'd have a falling out, silent treatment, this sort of shit. A lot of times I found myself apologising when I didn't really know what it was for.

As soon as I finished competing it was happy, happy that night. Next night I would go and get my medal, and all of a sudden, just like that, Kirsten had changed. She wouldn't talk to me. I'd hardly see her. Kristen's husband, Pat, was in Beijing as part of the Cook Islands team, coaching a discus thrower. I thought maybe she was torn between the two, because usually we'd hang out all the time at a major champs, and now Pat was here. I understood completely, and it should have been no big deal. But I would have appreciated it if maybe we'd talked about it.

We were rooming together at the village, but there was just nothing. However, I didn't let it ruin my experience. I was going out to see my family who were there. I went to the Great Wall of China with Visa. I saw my manager, Nick Cowan. I went to see other people compete, to the kayaking, the rowing, going everywhere, left, right and centre.

When I saw Kirsten I'd say, 'How's it going?' She'd hardly reply.

I came back one day and she was lying on the bed with Pat, sleeping, which I thought was kind of bizarre, because this was our room, with the bed right next to mine. I was just, 'Hi, bye.' Left the room. She was just really weird.

We had the same manager, Raylene, so I asked, 'What's going on?' She said just to carry on. 'Don't let it ruin your time here.'

I wished I could think of ways to make it better, to make Kirsten feel better. They had a beauty parlour in the village, so I went out and bought her a voucher for a massage, manicure and pedicure. I was trying everything I could to make her happy. She was very grateful, and said thank you very much. Later on she told me she was feeling torn over how to divide her time. That was at the end, and after that chat we were sweet.

That night the New Zealand team had a party, we had a

good time and then we left the next day.

It was the biggest competition of my life, so I was excited, jumping out of my skin. At the same time it was an anticlimax. All that pressure and adrenalin running through your body, and then it's all gone, so you hit a stage where you can feel sad, feel a bit depressed for a few hours. That sort of shit.

The next day you realise, 'Oh my God, it's so awesome, you've done this for your country.' Lots of emotions.

I came back home and my back was shot. All that tension had been running through my body and then all of a sudden I'm all relaxed. The whole time at the Games I was tense. There was not a moment when I let go. At training and when I wasn't training. Problems with Kirsten. Problems with Bertrand. When I got back home I had an MRI, which showed my back had turned to custard. I had four compressed discs and a bulging one.

I had two weeks at home and then I had to go back to Europe to compete in the world final. I wasn't sure if I was going to make it onto the plane or not. I continued to train to keep my body in shape and just to keep it going. I saw Lou, my physio, every day, often twice a day, and we did everything we could to warm it up, to loosen it up. Doing cat and camel exercises on the ground, all these weird exercises to loosen and stretch the back.

Then I had to see Dr Graham Paterson to obtain a clearance to go. I had to touch my toes without any pain. I had lots of sciatic pain, bloody painful. But I passed the test and was able to go.

So I flew to London via Los Angeles. Every hour, on the hour, I was stuck between two toilet doors inside the plane doing cat and camels on the floor, trying to keep my back as free as possible.

The Air New Zealand people were very nice to me. If it was free in business class, they would have upgraded me, but it was full, so I flew economy. The pain was at its worst when I was standing up or sitting. It was better when I was lying down.

On a 12-hour flight I was on the floor doing exercises, seven or eight times. People must have been looking and thinking, 'What the hell?' I didn't care. I really didn't. There I was on the floor, looking like a real dick, on all fours, arching my back, sticking my butt out, and then stretching up. It does look funny, but I had to do it.

When I got to Italy at the first stop in Rovereto, every morning and every night, every chance I got, I was doing the exercises. Half press-ups, too, trying to loosen up my back. I was in a little hotel, and every chance I got I was on the ground.

I competed, and I won the competition.

As much pain as you can imagine, I was in it. I got that beautiful anti-flam stuff that heats up your back. I used a whole tub. I smelt like freakin' menthol, but I didn't care. I was there to compete, and the meet manager was going to pay me, so I was going to do it.

So I competed. I threw 19.75 metres and I won the competition. Then I went to Stuttgart in Germany, mentholed myself up, cat and camelled, and I won. Lot of pain, but I won.

Everyone was still on a high with the Olympics, so I managed to get upgraded from Los Angeles to Auckland, which was really good, because I could lie down. But by the time I got home my back was worse. I was only home for a week, and I was supposed to be taking my sister Paddy to Rarotonga for a week's holiday.

Lou tried to do her magic. Massage, heat pads, soft tissue, acupuncture, all the rest of it. You name it, she was onto it.

Three days before Rarotonga I was a bit stiffer. I looked like I had a carrot up my bum. Second day the carrot grew bigger. The morning I was leaving to go to Rarotonga I couldn't stand up properly and it looked like I had a massive courgette.

The pain was hell. Every time I moved, every time I bent, every time I coughed or sneezed, it hurt.

Lou said to me, 'That's the sort of the feeling you get when you have a baby.' I thought, 'Mmm, maybe I don't want to have a baby any more.'

I drove from Botany, where I was living then, to my sister's house, went to the airport, and by the time we got to the airport I was bent over. We checked in and went upstairs to the departure area, and by this time my sister was saying, 'Let's just not go.' I said, 'No, we're going.'

She went and asked for airport help, and they said, 'Do you want a wheelchair?' I was having a hard time breathing, trying to keep a straight face. I lay down on the floor in a foetal position. I rang up my physio: 'Lou, please, help me. My pain's gone right down my back to my ankle.'

They put me in a bloody wheelchair. A freakin' Olympic champion three weeks before and now I'm wheeled to the plane in a wheelchair.

The airport help man said, 'Ma'am, would you like a wheelchair?' I was like, 'No.' Being a stubborn cow, holding onto the desk to stay still. He was saying, 'Are you sure, ma'am?' Paddy's whispering, 'It's okay Sis, just get a wheelchair.' Finally, in a little, tiny voice, I said, 'Okay, get a wheelchair.'

I was so bloody embarrassed I pulled my hoodie over my head. I'd said to Paddy, 'I'll crawl on my hands and knees to the plane.' She carried all our bags, while I was in the wheelchair, then I had to get off it to go through Customs.

Thank God the plane wasn't full. The people on the Air New Zealand flight were really nice. They said, 'Come up the front, sit up here.' It was the first time Paddy had been in business class, she was so excited. 'Yay, we're in business class.' All I could do was mumble, 'Okay. Okay.'

When the plane was taking off I was heavy breathing as though I was in labour. There were four free seats at the back. As soon as it got up in the air I asked, 'Could I please go and lie down at the back?'

Lying down was better but it was still misery for me. Not for Paddy. She was coming back to tell me, 'Oh my God, they've got so much food up there. It's so stink you can't come up and enjoy it with me.' I just said, 'You go up and enjoy it.'

While the plane was in the air my physio rang my doctor, he rang up Rarotonga, and in the four hours we were travelling he'd arranged things so that when I arrived in Rarotonga they had a whole bunch of drugs waiting for me.

When we finally got to Rarotonga I was a little bit better, happy to be there, where it was so warm. Paddy got all our stuff. I walked out, my brother was there waiting for us, and we went straight to his house. The best thing was that the doctor came to the house with some painkillers.

We arrived at about 2 pm and I was in pain for the next few hours. But by 8 pm I was at the pub, dancing away until 4 am. The secret? Drugs. I'd had a little sleep. When I woke up I thought, let's go, forget this shit.

I didn't have any alcohol that night because the drugs are pretty heavy, but I had a great time. It didn't ruin the holiday, so for 10 days it was fantastic.

The main problem was a bulging disc hitting the nerve. I have been doing heavy lifting from quite a young age, which is not necessarily very good for you if your core strength is not good. Olympic squatting and lifting is pretty hard on the old body.

I was as strong as an ox, but my core strength wasn't that great, nor was the stability within the core, so more pressure was going on my spine. I was strong everywhere else, but I was clearly a little bit overweight, and my back didn't function that well.

Coming home was fine. The hostess said, 'This is a great surprise.'

When I came back I had an MRI that confirmed there were four squashed discs and one bulging. The vertebra compresses and that squirts the ligaments and cartilage out of it, so it leaves bone on bone. It's quite nasty to have, and I was quite young to have that sort of problem.

I went to see the doctor and asked what the options were. There was always the option to have surgery, but to prolong not having that I wound up getting an injection like an epidural in my back. They put a needle with steroids straight into my back.

I had them on the S1 and the L5 vertebrae, on both left and right. That seemed to do the trick, but the problem was I was reliant on the injections. Every three months I'd get a jab.

To keep me going I had to have them. I'm taller than a lot of people, but although I'm quite solid for my height I should have developed other areas in my body when I was a little bit younger. In the last year I've only had one epidural, and that lasted the whole season. Lou was amazed it got me through the entire year. But I've worked so much harder on my core. It's so strong now that it can take the pressure off the back.

After being in Rarotonga I went to New Caledonia where Bertrand was with his parents, and we had a reconciliation.

While I was on holiday in Rarotonga, Kirsten had a holiday

with her family as well. We started back into training and it was actually okay, and Kirsten and I decided to go to Europe. Bertrand joined us, along with my physio, and we went to a place called Obernai in north-eastern France.

Then back in New Zealand, Bertrand and I lived together again. He qualified for the world champs in 2009, and we all went to the French nationals together and I won and he won, so it was good times.

But that was probably one of the hardest preparations for me because trying to please Bertrand and please Kirsten was a tough thing. I thought I did a pretty good job because I kept the peace.

Bertrand is very hard-headed, and I felt I was constantly apologising for him being himself. Kirtsen coached him and he qualified for the world champs in Berlin.

We went to Berlin for the 2009 world champs. Lou the physio was my outlet while we were away. When I had my massages with her I'd talk about everything. Let loose, so to speak.

In the competition I was the favourite to win, and, of course, that puts on the pressure. It didn't go as smoothly as I wanted it to. I was chasing from the word go.

After the third round I was in fifth place. I'd thrown 19.40 metres. I was looking over to Kirsten for something, anything, that might get me up more. I could see she was stressing, because that was the first time she or I had been put into that situation.

Did she know what to do? I don't know, but I was shitting myself big time. But I knew I was strong, and I came through in the fifth round and I threw 20.25 metres to take the lead.

Naturally, I was relieved. In the last round I threw 20.44 metres and I was ecstatic that I'd won, but it was the most stressful competition ever.

Kirsten and I were rooming together. Same old. Leading up was really good, but then, after I won, boom, silent treatment again. It happened only for a couple of days, but it was fairly obvious. She was hardly talking. I really don't know why. Maybe it's how she deals with things. I really don't know, but I find it a bizarre way. Especially when we've won, and it feels like a great thing, and all the rest of it.

We had drinks and stuff afterwards, and then, you know, she went a little quiet again.

Maybe it was because Bertrand was there. It is different having a partner with you, because you're trying to keep things happy in the relationship while you're also trying to concentrate on what you're doing. It gets even more complicated when you've both got the same coach.

When Kirsten's not happy with Bertrand she's telling me, and I'm thinking, 'Don't tell me about it. He's a big boy, I'm not his mother. Go and talk to him.'

After Berlin we competed in some small meets in Germany and most of the time we were fine. I think the breaking point was in March 2010 when I lost in Doha (the capital of Qatar on the Persian Gulf), in the 2010 world indoor championships.

I competed and I lost my first title in two years. When that happened I was upset, but I was still happy that I had managed to throw 20.49 metres. When we came back there was a lot of publicity about me losing. Kirsten and I basically stopped talking for two weeks, which wasn't good as we were due to go to the nationals.

I would go to a training session and Kirsten would just hand me a written programme, and I'd train, and I would leave.

I didn't turn up to a couple of sessions, when I was slightly injured, and once when I had to. When I arrived at the last session in Auckland before we were heading down to Christchurch, I didn't know things were going to turn out the way they did.

I had a small suspicion Kirsten was going to break up with me, but I didn't really buy into it. I still thought we could work our way through it. Maybe I'm naive. But she wasn't talking to me at all. I mean totally ignoring me. I'd speak and there would be no reply. It was almost like I had to beg for her attention, or her praise.

After training when I went home, I thought, 'That was a bit weird.' But when I left, Kirsten did say, 'Okay, see you in Christchurch.'

I didn't know then that I was going to meet her that afternoon. I rang up my manager, Nick, and asked him what he thought was going on. Kirsten, I'd find out, wanted to tell me after nationals that she wanted to break it off. She wanted to coach me at nationals, and then tell me after the competition down there.

On reflection I thought that was kind of selfish. What did she expect my reaction to be? To be happy? To have a party? Of course not, I'm going to be torn apart.

What it would mean was hopping back on the plane, flying back on my own with no support around me. She had her whole family around her, but I had no one. We were staying at the same place, so if she hadn't told me, and I was assuming we were all good, I would have felt a bit stupid if after being cold to me for three days at nationals she then told me she wasn't coaching me any more.

We had a meeting at Waipuna Hotel. Nick came along with my lawyer, Maria. I was as nervous as fuck. Then Kirsten and Pat turned up.

Everybody walked in with a cold sort of look, and I was much the same. I didn't know what to do. You need somebody who's thinking clearly, and not so heavily emotionally involved, which is why we thought having Maria there to mediate was a sensible idea. She is really good at trying to sort things out.

I did not walk in with my lawyer and manager saying to Kirsten, 'You get out of my life.' Not at all.

Nick was there as my support, and Maria was there purely to mediate. I didn't have anyone there for support otherwise. Kirsten had her husband. My husband, Bertrand, was in New Caledonia.

At first we all went together into a room. Then Kirsten and I were left alone. She did almost all the talking. She told me she didn't want anyone else involved, she wanted it to be just me and her. I was thinking, 'Yeah, that's fine, but who do I have?' At the end she said, 'I hope we can still be friends.' I didn't give much of an answer. I was upset, and was very quiet.

It wasn't the first time the idea of parting company had been discussed. But it was never presented to me as 'You need a change', it was always, 'If you want we can break up'.

My translation, how I felt about it, was that it felt like a guilt trip. It was never 'You need some more expertise', it was 'If you want to' which is a totally different line, and changes the whole complexion of the discussion.

At Waipuna Hotel Kirsten was angry and upset that Nick and Maria had become involved. She wanted to be able to tell me on our own down in Christchurch. But after that she would go back to her hotel room and her husband and children would be there. I'd go back to my hotel room, and nobody would be there.

She said at the meeting that she would still coach me through the nationals. I was thinking, 'How the fuck is that going to work? Are you serious? You tell me you're going to split up, but you'll still coach me through the nationals?'

Then everyone else came in and they talked about how they were going to announce it, and Kirsten got pretty angry. I think she was more upset at them than she was at me. She and Pat got up and left. It was quite upsetting. I had a big cry with Nick, then went home and rang up Paddy, and rang a couple of good friends and had a talk about it with them.

I got Nick to fly down to Christchurch on the day I was competing, so we could fly back together. At nationals I felt a little weird. Okay at times, out of place at others. Mostly, I just felt really awkward.

I just couldn't see how Kirsten could coach me at nationals. I tried to be as positive and normal as possible on the Friday. I picked up the car at the airport, found the place I was staying, and went and trained at the track. I could see Kirsten there, but we didn't talk. I just went to the back of the ground, did what I had to do and went home. We had never actually agreed that she wouldn't coach me at nationals, but she didn't come anywhere near me, and I didn't go to her.

When I competed, I was trying my hardest, but I was so upset that in the fourth round I put my dark glasses on, because I was starting to cry. Kirsten and her family were in the crowd. What the hell do I do? The only person in the competition who knew what was happening was a friend, Sarah Cowley. I had to tell someone.

I threw like crap the whole time, crying through the last three rounds, and when the competition finished I asked the reporters if I could have a few minutes to compose myself.

They asked me about Doha, and then about the nationals. I told them, 'I was a little bit off the pace today,' trying to give them something. As soon as it was over I left the track with Nick, went to the airport and flew back home.

The next day, a Sunday, I recorded a one-on-one interview with Eric Young at Prime TV, and then I had a press conference at five o'clock at the Millennium Institute of Sport, where I do a lot of my training. I read out a statement and I took questions. I was upset the whole time. I was on the verge of tears. We'd agreed at the meeting at Waipuna we'd say it was a mutual decision to split. That was what I said at the press conference, and I kept my word.

Later, Kirsten was on TVNZ's *Close Up*, saying that it was my decision. And I thought, 'Shit, this going to get bitter,' and it was. We hardly spoke for ages, although there was the odd text. It feels weird now every time I'm around her. It feels pretty artificial to me. 'Great to see you, how are things?' 'Yeah, good thanks.' We don't see each other socially at all.

When I found out Kirsten was coaching the Chinese girl, Li Ling, I thought, what you did with me worked on me, but I'm not quite sure it's going to work with Li Ling. At first I didn't care. I felt it's your choice, if China's where you want to be.

In 2011 at the world champs, Kirsten, for me, was basically training the enemy. It's not a personal thing. When I'm competing I'm there to kick your ass, not to be friendly. I'm not sure Kirsten realised how dramatically our relationship had changed.

At the world champs it was bizarre. With the Chinese throwers it's like there's two camps for me. Kirsten trains Li Ling, and the coach of the other top thrower, Lijiao Gong, is really nice, she's a friend of mine. They call me Walarie, because they can't say 'V'. It was worse when I was Valerie Vili. They'd say, 'Hey, Miss Wili, Miss Wili, how are you?'

After the break with Kirsten I was in a bit of a panic. Didier Poppe was the only option. He had been a French national coach, before moving to Auckland, where he coaches Jacko Gill. I asked Nick to approach Didier and he said he'd take me on. I trained with him from April 2010, until the end of the season in September.

Didier was a tough cookie. He does things his own way. He tried to change me, he told the media, from a truck to a Ferrari. I wondered about that. If you want to train a Ferrari, you should probably have a 100 metres sprinter. But that was how he described it.

For me he was a difficult man to work with. It was his way, or no way. He mapped out a programme for me, but it was a generic programme. I was older and vastly more experienced than I had been when I started with Kirsten, but remember Didier was only my second coach. I was in panic mode, and I had to trust him. He sounded like he had everything planned and ready to go.

But, eventually, I felt that technically Didier broke what I'd achieved, and improved on, with Kirsten. He made the base of my throw wider, he had different ways of throwing, and it didn't work with me.

The things he was asking me to do weren't improving me. He wanted to get my base wider, he was hell bent on my left leg being lower. I felt that instead of breaking me down we should be working on building up what I already had. In fact, technically, I was broken.

Suddenly, instead of being able to throw 20 metres every time I went out to throw, I was now struggling to get to 20 metres.

I just had a crap year, the worst I'd ever had. We had a training camp in a small place called Evreux in France. It was hell. The place we stayed in was shit, where we trained was no better, and every day going to training was a struggle. I knew in my heart that this was crap, but I had to keep going because I didn't have anyone else to go to.

I struggled in every competition, but the one thing I didn't let down was to get lower than second place. When I threw 20 metres it was a cause for big celebration, and, really, on my past record, it shouldn't have been.

The breakthrough in 2010 came when I had a 10-day gap after my last Diamond League meet and Didier went to Singapore to a youth Olympics, where he was working with Jacko Gill.

I had the chance to go to Jean-Pierre Egger for 10 days. In 10 days, I swear to God, we did six throw sessions, which is a lot in that time. He said, 'You're so wide, why are you so wide?' I was in the competition phase, so I was still quite dynamic, I still had something there.

So we threw and we threw, we did a few contrast dynamic lifting sessions. But on the technique side he just hammered me for six sessions.

I went to the IAAF (International Association of Athletics Federations) world cup in Split, Croatia in September, and I threw 20.70 metres, then 20.86, 20.76, 20.56, the best series of my life, after 10 days with Jean-Pierre. He was the first person I texted. I was so excited, and I still had the Commonwealth Games in Delhi to come a month later.

I asked Jean-Pierre his opinion on what I should do for the next three weeks, and he said no problem, do these sessions for the next three weeks, then add a bit more weight, come down a little, and then peak.

When I got home I told Didier what I wanted to do, the technical aspects that I'd learnt. Now we were butting heads the whole time, while we were in Singapore, preparing for the Commonwealth Games. I'd learned something from Jean-Pierre that worked. It was obvious it had worked. I told Didier what I wanted to do, and I was so determined that I wanted to do it that Didier didn't like it.

He wrote an email to Jean-Pierre asking, 'What did you do to Valerie?' So I thought, 'You're questioning how I got so good, and why I'm not hanging on every word like I was before.'

I was adamant that this is what I was going to do. So I did it. I did some of Didier's exercises just to please him. But in the technique sessions we were at loggerheads all the time. We argued over what I wanted to do. I didn't mind going to the gym with him, but the throwing sessions were hell. It was so hard.

From there we went to Delhi and the same shit happened. I just did it my way. It was the last competition of the year for me, so it had to be a good one.

Didier wasn't very happy with me doing things my way. I didn't want to overstretch, and some of the things he'd brought in were pushing me to do more than I wanted to do. I was very headstrong; I just said, 'No, I don't want to do that.' It was freaking hot in India, so it didn't take me long to warm up.

I competed, and I threw really well. My left leg was good, so was my back leg, and all my throws were over 20 metres. The best was 20.47 metres and I won the gold. It was fine then.

When I came home it was over with Bertrand, and that led to the final split with Didier. He'd gone over to France, and he'd told some people there my brothers wanted Bertrand to go back to New Caledonia feet first — a French expression meaning he'd go back in a coffin. Totally untrue. The athletics community isn't that big, even in France. So everybody knew about it. I heard it from a very reliable source.

I rang up Nick and I was so pissed off I said, 'I'm not going to train with him any more.' We had a meeting, and I was willing to get his side of the story. I asked him, and he denied it for about 15 minutes. Then he said, 'I might have said something like that.' I said, 'So you did say it?' I said to Nick, 'We're done.'

At this stage, when I say I'm moving on to my third coach, the media are bagging me, and Sparc start getting on my case asking if the money is being well spent, if they're going to be losing any more on it, why is she changing again, what's happening with her?

Someone from Sparc even wanted to come and see me train. I was offended by that. Why couldn't they just look at the results? Who would know best what someone needs as a thrower — the thrower or someone sitting in an office?

In the end, I had two weeks on my own. In the one month of November my goal was to lose weight. That was when I started working with the Sports Academy boys, Matt and Mike, the strength and conditioning coaches. They got me into shape. I lost 15 kilograms in a month, and got myself strong and really fit at the same time. I had to work really hard.

While that was happening we were working things out with Jean-Pierre. I was making phone calls, asking if he'd take me on.

Eventually, he said he would, so I trained up to 24 December, and then at the beginning of January I went over to Switzerland.

6

When a house is not a home

The night of the Halberg Awards of 2006 should have been a happy occasion for me and my husband Bertrand Vili.

For the first time I was nominated for New Zealand Sportswoman of the Year, and Bertrand and I were together at a function where the biggest names in sport socialise together. I was just hoping nobody would ask too much about the white plaster on Bertrand's hand, a reminder to me of the massive problems that would eventually break our marriage apart.

Just two nights before the Halbergs he'd been drinking outside our home with neighbours and some other friends he'd invited.

When I went to bed I said to him, 'Please. If you drink, stay, don't go out in the car.' He said, 'Sure babe, I'll just stay here.'

My bedroom is next to the carport and he was blasting music from the car's sound system. Eventually, I went to sleep, because it had gone silent.

I wake up and I get a phone call and I don't hear any music outside. It's Bertrand; he's had a car accident. My heart is pumping like mad, just about jumping out of my chest. I hop in my little Daihatsu and dash to where he is.

He'd written off the V8 Holden, could have possibly killed

the people in the car. He'd gone too fast at a roundabout, smashed a barrier open, and gone into a garden in Howick. He was 399 micrograms per litre of breath, which was one microgram under the drunk-in-charge limit for alcohol. The police were there, and an ambulance had been called.

Five people were in the car, and they had a chilly bin full of beer. The one thing I'd always asked was to not drink and drive. 'If you want to go out, don't take the car.'

But despite what had happened he was calm. He even seemed to think somehow he was the man. I was so upset I swear I nearly wet my pants.

He had to go to the police station in the early hours of the morning, and he was still being all cool. Two of his mates had run away because they were scared of the cops coming. He had a small cut on his hand so that night was spent at the police station and then at accident and emergency getting the cut attended to.

The morning after the crash I had physio and I went to Lou Johnson and all I did was cry and tell her what had happened. She rang up my coach, Kirsten, to tell her what had happened to warn her, and I put on a happy face for the Halberg Awards two days later.

Some weeks later we went to court, which was the first time in my life I'd ever been in one. Bertrand was charged with dangerous driving. I was the most embarrassed person in there. It was almost like he was walking around as if he was a cool dude.

He was disqualified for six months. This should have been a wake-up call for him, but it wasn't. But the risks weren't big enough to stop him.

We all have an idea of what marriage is going to be like, but even if you know it won't all be romantic and lovely, I know I had hopes for a normal life, with respect and friendship. Sadly, it was rarely like that for Bertrand and me.

Bertrand and I met in 2001 at a track and field meet in New Caledonia called the four throws competition (the shot, discus, javelin and hammer), where I won my section and he won his.

One of my throws wasn't so good and I said 'dick' in Tongan. It's kind of a rude slang word in Tongan, and I didn't realise many New Caledonians can understand Tongan, until they all turned around and looked in horror, because they all knew what I'd said.

Bertrand's mum and dad were originally from Uvea in the French territory of Wallis and Futuna. It was part of the Tongan empire from the thirteenth to the sixteenth century, and so the locals began speaking Tongan there. As a tribute, so the legend goes, the Tongans were given three big rocks, 20-tonne coral slabs, which are now a tourist attraction at Ha'amonga 'a Maui in Tonga.

Since the nineteenth century Wallis and Futuna has been under French control, and the language has evolved, but there are still many words that are the same as Tongan.

So that was our first interaction, not that great I suppose. He and his friends all had a little giggle, and then we had the awards ceremony in the afternoon. We went our own ways, but the day after we spoke on the phone very briefly. When I went back home we started writing to each other.

That was how our friendship started. We had a long-distance relationship for about two years before he eventually came over to New Zealand.

He was a good-looking guy, and a very good athlete, a discus thrower. I thought he was cute. I didn't really know what sort of person he was until we got married. Before then he was a nice guy, and his family seemed pleasant when I went back to Noumea and met them.

We weren't living together, but we were dating. He was my first love, my first real boyfriend. It wasn't love at first sight, but the relationship grew, and after two years I wanted to make it work and he moved to Auckland.

At first things seemed to be going alright. He moved over here at the beginning of 2004, and I started training for the Olympics. We started living together, and I started to see some sort of aggressiveness then. But I tried to look ahead.

Bertrand went to France to train, and while he was away I got appendicitis. It was painful in itself, but it became more painful because I wanted to go to the Olympics, and he said, 'Don't go. You should stay home.' I said, 'But I want to go. The doctor says I can go, and I want to try.' Finally, he came around, but it took a lot of convincing. When we were talking I was crying my ass off over the phone, after surgery, feeling sorry for myself. It was the pits.

After two days of silence he said, 'Okay, you can go.' Obviously, I felt better about that. So I went to the Games in Greece, finished eighth, and the day I came back home from Europe we went home to the house we were renting, and that's when he proposed.

I was very happy. I'd missed him while he was away. I thought maybe in one year or two years we'd get married. But he wanted to get married, 'snap', right away. It took me a while to come around to that idea, but eventually I did. I came home in September, and we tied the knot on 27 November 2004.

It was a trying time. I was really young, I'd just turned 20, and it took some getting used to. You think it'll be forever. I went to classes so we could get married in the Catholic Church.

Later, if we were having a barney, he'd say, 'Don't forget the promise we made in front of God.'

In hindsight I realise Bertrand didn't pay for anything. His birthday is 6 September, and he wanted me to wear a ring at his birthday party. I ended up buying my own engagement ring for about $700. That was a sign as well. He asked me to marry him but he had nothing to offer, not even a romantic gesture. I felt a bit sorry for myself, because it wasn't the loving dream. We went out for his birthday to Valentines, told everybody we were getting married, and everyone was happy.

Come the wedding day and Kirsten and her family organised a lot of things. Bertrand did bugger all, and the only thing that was really mine was my dress, because I didn't want white. I wanted it really simple, so we found a dressmaker and got that done. I ended up buying both wedding rings, and paying for his suit hire and his father's suit hire. That should have been a hint, too, right? But I still had the hope that this was not going to be the case in the future.

For the reception Kirsten and Pat kindly put the bill on their Visa card, and I paid them back later. So, basically, I paid for the wedding. The only part Bertrand and his father contributed was to pay the priest some money. That was interesting.

As soon as we got married, things turned. By January 2005, I kicked him out of the house, we separated and he went back to New Caledonia.

Nobody knew what had happened. I played two lives, making out to people things were okay, especially when it was anything to do with him. I was getting good at making excuses for Bertrand.

Why did I hide what was going on? I was so afraid of the judgements I would receive because of what had happened, or

I was trying to protect him, or I was trying to make it work for us. Somehow I was able to hide it from the press, anything that was happening.

We'd been renting a small place, and then we moved, and it was really turning to custard. I kept encouraging him to get a job. But he was a very slow mover, not very motivated to get a job to help us, not driven to assist. It frustrated me for a very long time.

We'd moved to the new place just before Christmas. Things got rocky, and then he took off, for the first time. We had a barney, and I went to bed. When I woke up in the morning I walked outside and found all the wheels on the car had been scraped.

That was the first time I went to my sister's house. He tried to stop me in the bedroom, but I basically got in the car, ran it down the drive and stayed the night at my sister's.

Then starts the 'I'm sorry, I'm sorry, I love you' on the phone. At one stage I actually turned the phone off. But, eventually, he reeled me in, and I went back.

A week later the same shit happened, but it was twice as bad. I came home from work one day, and he'd told his father to come over, to try to fix what was happening. His father turned up to try to patch up a marriage he wasn't involved in. His father was sitting there, and I tried to keep a straight face, but it just wasn't working out.

They'd sleep in the lounge and I'd sleep in my room, and then in the morning I'd go to work at Macleans College.

The father didn't know about his son's drinking; he saw it as a global problem with the two of us. His family are very religious, and it seemed their answer was to pray a lot, to ask God to help. I felt God's not going to help, he's not going to stop Bertrand drinking, he's the one who picks up the bottle and puts it in his mouth.

One morning I'd hardly slept, and Bertrand had been pestering me all night. I just told him to please leave me. I was crying most of the night under the blankets, and then I got up, took off my wedding rings and put them on the shelf.

In the morning I woke up early, got my pushbike that I went to work on at Macleans College, went to Kirsten's place, and hid the bike behind her house.

He'd woken up and came to Kirsten's, saying, 'Where the fuck is Valerie? I want to talk to her. I want to talk to my wife.'

That was the last straw. I bought him and his father tickets to go home. I put them in the letterbox. Then when they left I moved out of the house and put my stuff in storage and was living where I could.

In March we had no contact. In May I organised my dad's reunion. I was still very mad, up until the world champs in Helsinki in August. Then he tried to do the sorry stuff again, and he reeled me back in. He was a very good fisherman.

I had finished third in Helsinki. I put a hyphen in my name at the world champs, I was Adams-Vili there and nobody really picked up on it, maybe because I was a newly-wed, and they thought I was still adjusting to the name change.

After the world champs he worked his charm, and before you know it, we were back together.

In 2006 it began as an okay year, but I was still pushing for Bertrand to get a job. He was still training on his own, but not working. When we moved into another house, all of a sudden he wanted a big car. I'd saved up a bit of money, because my goal in life was always to buy a house. His goal was a car.

The first bit of money I had, with some money from the world champs in 2005, was enough to buy a Holden Clubsport V8. Big car. But then he wanted a sound system in it, wanting to be cool.

That was the car he wrecked at the Howick roundabout. Because he was just inside the legal drink-driving limit the insurance company paid for the car. Now he wanted a bigger, better car. When he sulked, had a hissy fit, I'd give in, to keep the peace. I hated having that atmosphere in the house, and by the start of 2007 he'd got a new Holden.

Looking back, I think as I got better at my sport, and I was having more success, he got worse. The jealousy grew. Usually, in a household the man is the head honcho, bringing home all the bacon. All he was bringing in was bills, wanting the biggest car and the biggest music blasting out of it.

So as time went on he got worse, and the worst year was before the 2008 Olympics. His career wasn't going well, and mine was taking off.

After the Olympics I tried to help him qualify for the world champs, and eventually we did that. But 2008 was the worst year of my life with him.

His drinking came to be three or four nights a week until the early hours of the morning. One night I came home from training and he was already gone. I was waiting for the police to turn up. I was barely sleeping, keeping one eye open, tired as hell. Every night he'd go out I was waiting for the cops to come and tell me he was dead, to go and identify the body.

He gave no consideration to the fact I was training for the biggest competition of my life. He was very jealous that so much of my time was spent at training. He wanted to get back at me, and he knew his behaviour hurt me, and it did. While he was drinking, who was paying for it? For his petrol, for his drink?

At the same time I didn't want that to wreck my dreams as an athlete. I went to every function I was asked to go to. I went to every press conference as if nothing had happened, and I acted as if I was all good. But hardly anybody knew what I was living with at home.

Nick, my manager, knew about it, Kirsten and Pat knew about it, and Paddy my sister knew about it, but nobody else did. I kept it straight, and I kept it going, and I kept the image going.

I'd come home to a house full of negative shit. I'd go to training and come back, empty house, the house is dirty, and there's no food. All he was doing was drinking, and worrying about his car.

We separated. I went down to Kirsten's house for a few nights. I did a drive-by at our house and there were three or four cars there, and people playing Xboxes and stuff in my lounge, having a drink.

I was thinking to myself, 'You're such a coward.' I'd had it up to the brim, and in June I'd bought him a ticket and told him to eff off back home.

I rang up his mum after I told him to go back home. She wasn't any help to me. She never got on the phone to tell him to pull his head in. He was always the sparkle in his parents' eyes.

He trashed the house. The morning I came over to pick him up and take him to the airport he'd just got home half an hour before.

But after the Olympics he reeled me back in. He could be charming at the right time, and when he got upset it really hurt me. At the end of 2008 he worked his charm, and his family worked theirs. He was in Noumea and I eventually went over in October and, before you know it, we're playing big happy families again.

We came back home in 2008. Then he started to train with Kirsten, heading into the 2009 world champs. He was a bit slack at first, still drinking every now and again. But then he started to train seriously, and we ended up going to Europe together.

When we went to Europe he didn't have any money, so I said, 'Join my camp,' and we shared a room in France, and went to the French nationals where he won.

The French team for the world championships was selected and he was in it. It was the first time he'd been involved in the preparation with me before a major championship, and it was hard. He wanted everything his way. I was piggy in the middle with him and Kirsten, and my only outlet was Lou Johnson, the physio, who was with us.

So I did what I had to, went to Berlin, and I won, staying with the New Zealand team. He stayed with the French team, and that was alright.

After we competed he went off his face and started drinking, but then a lot of people were doing that after they'd competed.

When we came home in 2009 I said to him, 'You need to get a job.' We argued a lot, and things could erupt anywhere. I remember going to the Cock & Bull pub, and he told me, 'You can't tell me I can't go out with my friends. I'll go out with them if I want to.' He's the type of guy that'll make a scene anywhere; he wouldn't give a shit who was watching. His voice was getting louder and louder and I got embarrassed. I'd won the Olympics and people were starting to recognise me.

Somehow we worked through that and ended up buying a house in Half Moon Bay at the end of 2009. He didn't have a cent to put into the house, but I was able to buy it and move in on 19 December.

But now we had the house, he wanted the car to fit the house, and his ego seemed to grow. He said, 'I'll sell this Holden and buy another car.' I was thinking, 'Why? Every time you sell and buy another car, we're losing money.'

He wants music in the car, amplifiers that cost thousands of dollars. They're not an investment, just a waste of money.

We have Christmas at the house, and I'm trying to enjoy living there as best I can.

At the start of 2010 the problems get worse between Kirsten and me. We went to the world indoors, and things with Bertrand were okay, not great. At the world indoors I lost. He wasn't so sympathetic to me losing, but so it goes.

Then the news broke that Kirsten and I were parting company. I was going to Rarotonga for a friend's wedding after the nationals in Christchurch. I wanted a break. Bertrand wanted to go to New Caledonia because he didn't want to stay home by himself.

When the break with Kirsten became public he rang up and started going crazy, cursing about Kirsten. I said I was okay. I'd find it hard to say which side he was on.

I'd been to Rarotonga, but Bertrand was still in Noumea when I decided to work with Didier Poppe. As soon as Bertrand found out he called me:

'What are you going to Didier for? You know I don't like him. You know we have history and I really don't want you to go with him.'

'What do I do?'

You choose between me and him.'

I kept training with Didier and eventually Bertrand came back from New Caledonia. I went away to Taiwan and New York by myself to compete, and when I was in Taiwan he rang and said he wanted me to ask Didier to coach him.

I knew their history, that they hated each other. I spoke to Didier and he said, 'No, never. I won't train with him.'

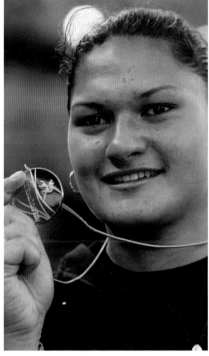

Above: My first placing at a senior world championship came in 2005 in Helsinki, when I was 20 years old. Russia's Olga Ryabinkina (left) won silver, Nadzeya Ostapchuk won gold, and I finished with bronze.

Left: Gold in the 2006 Commonwealth Games in Melbourne. Happy memories: a new Games record, good friends in the big track team, and getting to know the Silver Fern netballers, a really cool, humble group.

Right: At the 2007 world champs in Osaka, I had to wait before my last throw and Kirsten Hellier called me. Dad had died in May of that year, and this was in August, and she said to me, 'Throw this one for your dad.' It was a bit of a risk, saying that, but it was a positive thing, and that was when I got amped up and threw a personal best.

Below: Enjoying my first world title, and a throw of 20.54 metres.

Celebrating with my family after winning the Halberg Sportsperson of the Year in February 2008.

No crowd, no cheers, but without hours of training like this, at Mt Smart Stadium in 2008, you'll never succeed.

The faces, all from the 2008 Olympics in Beijing. Let's start with the happy look.

Then competition begins and it's time for the good old 'South Auckland don't eff with me' expression.

In my own world, inside a circle 2.135 metres in diameter, concentrating everything on getting 4 kg of shot put out as far as my body can propel it.

I've thrown 20.56 metres, a personal best, but laughter, jumping and screaming must wait, until I know no other thrower is going to do better.

Now I can celebrate, first with coach Kirsten Hellier.

A New Zealand flag, thrown out of the crowd to me. Wherever you go in the world, there'll be a random Kiwi or two.

I cried so much when the New Zealand anthem played it was kind of embarrassing but, hey, you try to hold back so many emotions and memories.

Gold, the best feeling ever.

Photosport

Above: After Beijing I was honoured as supreme winner at the 2009 Halberg Awards.

Photosport

Right: In 2009 in Berlin I won another world championship, but it was the most stressful competition I've ever been in. For the first time as a favourite I was struggling from the first round.

Left: My nieces show Mum the Commonwealth gold medal I won in Delhi in 2010.

Below: A low point in 2010, a year from hell. I can't conceal my emotions at the press conference announcing Kirsten won't be coaching me any more.

I loved the India I found outside the 2010 Commonwealth Games village. Here's the pose made famous by Princess Diana in front of the Taj Mahal.

My best friend among the shot-putters, Cleopatra Borel-Brown, from Trinidad and Tobago, sneaked away with me before dawn and we got to ride elephants in Jaipur.

Loved the purple sari. How could I not buy it?

Bertrand asked what Didier had said, and I just said he didn't think it was a very good idea. I then went home and a month later I had to leave for Europe.

The last straw for me turned out to not be a big thing in itself, but it was enough to push me over the edge. In reality it was the nine years leading up to it that made me leave.

I'd sorted out his phone before I left for Europe. He had a BlackBerry, which I put onto my contract so we could stay in contact. At the airport my sister Paddy was there saying, 'Have a great time. I'll miss you. Keep in touch.' Bertrand came up, gave me a kiss and then walked away. I got a text saying, 'Sorry I couldn't say goodbye properly, but your sister was there.' I thought that was weird.

I got to Europe in the morning, and found my way to where I had to stay. I went out to dinner and he sent me a message, but my phone was in my bag.

Here's where it got really bizarre. I found the message about two hours later and replied. He sent me a text saying, 'Eff you, if you're going to ignore me when you're out with your friends, don't ever text me again.' Then he deleted me off his contacts.

I left it for two weeks. I finally got a long email message, 'I'm sorry, I love you darling.' So we're back on talking terms.

We start texting again. Same shit happens. 'If you're not going to reply to me, eff you.' This time I was at breakfast, and I'd forgotten to take my phone with me.

That was the breaking point. I thought: no more of this shit. I deleted him off my phone. I went to a training camp in Paris, and two weeks later I woke up in Normandy, and suddenly I'd had enough.

He'd emailed me for two weeks, every day, saying he loved me.

He'd call me and I didn't even answer the phone. I woke up in the middle of one night and thought, 'That's it Valerie. No more.' I took my wedding ring off and put it down, and that was it. On my own in the middle of nowhere, I'd just had it up to here.

I sent him an email saying, 'I can't do this any more. I'm done with this relationship. I'm done with you, and I don't want this marriage any more.'

I get a long email saying he loves me. Then he doesn't. Then he does.

He starts ringing around people. Calls his family. Two days later his mother's calling me, telling me I need to come back home, I need to fix this marriage. 'How dare you stay over there and tell my son the marriage is over?'

I think, 'No, I'm not married to you or your family. I married your prick of a son.'

By this stage after every single Diamond League meet I just got trashed, drank way too much. It was the only way that I felt good about myself. I was getting emotional abuse training with Didier.

I was trying to deal with all this emotional crap, working with a coach who was difficult to deal with, and at times it was my only outlet. I'd get trashed off my face, everywhere I went.

I'd ring my sister Paddy, and she was getting mad. She had seen what had gone on. She hadn't wanted to hurt me more, so she wouldn't try to interfere.

The person who was my refuge over there was Sandra, the French throwing coach. I needed someone to talk to directly. Over the phone is one thing, but talking to someone face to face they can see how you feel, what you feel.

When I really knew it was over was one night in London, talking to Paddy on Skype. My phone rings. It's Bertrand.

'Shall I answer it?'

'No, don't.'

'Nah, I'm gonna answer it.' I pick up the phone. 'Hello.'

'Please, please.'

'No, it's over.' I closed the phone, and it didn't hurt any more. When that happens there's no going back.

In New Zealand Bertrand visited my sister Paddy, and my little sister, Ana. And I'm thinking, 'What are you doing bro'? You didn't want to do that before, and now you want to get all lovey-dovey with them. Not going to work.'

He wanted me to be pregnant at the end of 2003. He said, 'Let's make babies now.' I think he wanted to be the first one in his family to produce a grandchild. I was still feeling that I could be someone, that I could go far in my sport.

He was adamant after Beijing in 2008 that we were going to have a baby. No. I wasn't ready. He thought I was going to get pregnant, but he didn't know that I was taking the pill.

The worst thing was that he wanted to control everything. If we were out in public and a guy came up to congratulate me, he wouldn't be happy. He was as jealous as hell. He got jealous of Nick my manager at one stage. I'm a friendly, talkative sort of person, but if a guy I knew from school said hello he'd be giving me the silent treatment on the way home, or saying, 'Who the hell was that?'

He couldn't see what was in front of his eyes — that the reason he could live like he did was because of the person he was trying to push away.

He'd get angry at nothing and punch holes in the walls. I was afraid of him and didn't know what he might do. It was an abusive situation. What I hated the most was being treated with silence. I find that almost impossible to deal with.

For some reason I felt sorry for him as a person. I think I believed that one day he would change. He'd change to be a normal guy, the guy that put food on the table. If he'd been 12 I could accept what he was doing. But he was in his twenties with no job, pissing around. On 24 July 2010 I sent him an email, which became the date of separation.

He wanted to see me when I got back to New Zealand. I wanted him out of my house. He said he wasn't going. He said, 'This is my house as well.' He fought to the bitter end.

I came home from Europe, and changed my flight so he wouldn't know when it was. I said to my manager Nick, 'Check the airport.' I was shit scared he was going to be there. My sister, the whole family was there. They got me in the car, and I went to Sky City and stayed there under a different name for a couple of weeks.

Eventually, we met at my sister Paddy's house, and he came in with his cousin. I was very, very nervous. He walked in, kissed me on the forehead, kissed Paddy, kissed Ana. He sat down and said, 'Babe, I don't know what's happening. I don't know why you're doing this to me. I'm really sorry. I hope we can make this work. You just send me emails saying it's over, and I don't know why.' I was thinking, 'What the hell? You don't know why?'

He kept on, and then I said, 'Are you finished?' By now I was teary. I said, 'Bertrand, I don't want to be with you any more. I don't love you any more, and I can't live with you. I don't want to be married to you, or be anywhere near you ever again. I'm sorry, but this is what I want.'

He goes, 'Okay, sweet then. I'll see you in court.'

I had a massive cry. I wasn't sure why I was so upset, but I suppose it was because, now, this was for real. I'd hyped myself up all day, and now it was five in the afternoon. It had all happened.

I'd already told my brother Rob what was happening, and all we heard half an hour later was 'boom, boom, boom' on the front door. My heart sank: 'Oh my God, who is it, who is it?'

Paddy opens the door. Nearly screams. 'Rob, you bloody bastard. I thought it was Bertrand.'

He goes, 'Yeah, I know.'

Rob had come all the way from Mt Maunganui, and had been sitting down the road, making sure nothing went wrong.

That was the last time I saw Bertrand.

When I came back from the Commonwealth Games in Delhi, he was still living in the house. But I was paying the mortgage. I found out he was on holiday in New Caledonia.

My lawyer said to me, 'You know you can move in.' I said, 'I'm not sure that I can.' She said, 'You can move in.' 'But if I do, does he have the right to come back?'

I left Sky City and lived at the lodge at the Millennium Institute of Sport in Mairangi Bay. I gave it a week, then I went to check out the house. The place was a tip, rubbish everywhere.

I got cleaners in. I went in on the Saturday with my sister and family, and I filled everything he owned in two rubbish bags. I put it in the truck I'd bought, which was still at the house.

I dropped his car off to a person he knew. I got the locks changed, security latches on every door. I lived in fear for about three months, with a baseball bat under my bed. I didn't know where he was.

When everything was signed, I knew I was free. I got my house blessed inside and outside, and for the first time I felt safe.

Before then the plants were all dead, even the lawn had died. I took all those out, planted new stuff, and now it's a garden. Now I'm not scared any more.

7

Tough choices

When I went to Switzerland to train with Jean-Pierre Egger in 2011 the first two months were horrible. I was very depressed.

Nothing to do with Jean-Pierre, or the work we were doing, that was all great. But being away from family, friends and New Zealand I felt isolated, and I felt more alone than I ever have in my life. I never actually wanted to give up, but so often I'd find myself wishing I could scoot over to New Zealand for the weekend and scoot back again.

Sometimes just out of the blue I'd be crying myself to sleep at night; I missed my family so much.

I was supposed to go to Switzerland in April for a couple of weeks and then return to New Zealand for a visit in June. The decision was made not to go because it would have been too hard to make sure I had a small peak for the Diamond League meet in Paris on 8 July.

I agreed with the choice for the sake of my performance, but it was a hard decision. I had to tell my family I wasn't going to be home, and every time I talked to them on Skype there was a lot of crying.

It was difficult. One night I was talking to my sister Paddy on the phone, and we were talking about something really funny. Then I just started crying and said, 'I've gotta go. I'll call you back in 10 minutes.' I called back and she said, 'Are you okay?' I said, 'Yeah . . . gulp, gulp . . . sniff . . . gulp . . . yeah.' Then *she* started crying. I thought, 'Aw shit.' We were just as bad as each other.

A lot of the Swiss athletes who train at Magglingen in Switzerland, where I'm based, leave on the Friday night and go back to their families, to their homes. In the weekends Magglingen is a dead place, a big-time ghost town, with no one around, probably just one worker down at reception and the chefs at the cafeteria.

After my parting with Didier Poppe I knew I wanted to work with Jean-Pierre. I rang him up and explained what had happened, then sent him an email. He took a couple of days to think about it, then kindly agreed to take up my coaching. Obviously, I couldn't expect him to give up his life in Switzerland and come to New Zealand to coach me. I basically had no choice but to go there, because it was what I had to do if I was going to continue as a shot-putter.

Jean-Pierre wasn't coaching anyone else at the time. He was very busy with the work he did with corporate team building. He might help a few athletes from other sports with strength and conditioning work, but he wasn't actually involved in athletics when I approached him.

Jean-Pierre works with the former world champion shot-putter Werner Gunthor. In Switzerland Werner is a household name. In track and field he's their biggest star, and he and Jean-Pierre are known to everyone there.

I live at the Swiss Olympic training centre. It's where Werner trained when he was an athlete. It's a massive place owned by the Swiss Government, situated on the top of a mountain. They have swimming, skiing, everything there.

Jean-Pierre and Werner had to talk to the Swiss officials for me to be allowed to go there and, fortunately for me, the relationship they have with the people at Magglingen is very good.

Werner works there, and Jean-Pierre brings a lot of his clients to the centre, where you work and eat and train.

They spoke to the bosses and they waived the fee to use the facilities, and helped me cut my costs renting the room I live in.

At the centre accommodation includes the Swiss Olympic House, the Bellavista Hotel, and military accommodation. In the Bellavista they have single bedrooms with a shower and a toilet. The military people are there for sport and fitness work, and where they stay there are shared showers and toilets for each floor.

I was able to stay in the Swiss Olympic House, where each room has a single bed, a TV, a toilet and a shower: the bare minimum. Not as flash as a hotel, more like a youth hostel with the luxury of a TV. I went and bought my own little fridge.

Including the bathroom and the toilet area, if you walk two steps you're at the other wall. There's no couch, just a chair for the small desk. When I first saw it I thought, 'I'll just adapt, and it'll be cool.'

After a while you do get claustrophobic, because I live in my own house in New Zealand, at Half Moon Bay. I have four bedrooms and a backyard, so there's room to stretch out. In Switzerland you really have to live in a very tidy, compact way, otherwise you just run out of space.

I have to hang my washing in my room. I wash in a laundry

that's near the dining room. They have dryers, but they don't really dry the clothes well, so I take them back and hang them up in my room. I sleep overnight with the aroma of detergent. Then, in the morning, hopefully they're dry enough for me to put them away.

I had to get used to it, and I had to make sure I wasn't getting so much stuff sent over I'd run out of space in my room.

I stored a lot of things in the car I leased from Mitsubishi. The people in New Zealand helped with that. If I needed anything I'd walk down to my car. Breakfast in the morning is seven to eight. No earlier, no later. Then lunch and dinner is at another building, Bellavista.

Scattered around are houses for long-term stay Swiss athletes, where it's almost like a flatting situation.

I was there for two and a half weeks in January 2011, then came back home for our summer season, then went back again in April for most of the year.

Fortunately, in April, late in the month, I was able to meet a Kiwi family: a lady called Royna, who's married to Cedi, a Swiss guy, and they live in Biel, a town at the bottom of the hill. The only reason I knew them was that their daughter's godmother was studying at Magglingen, and she found out I was from New Zealand, so she came to me and said they would like to invite me to have a meal.

So I got to know them. That helped a lot. At first I didn't want to impose, so I only went there every two weeks. Eventually, I became part of the furniture. They gave me a key, and now I just turn up.

It's still hard, though, because it's not your house, it's not your country, and when you know that you're only there for a certain length of time you don't start something permanent, or set up anything. You basically live out of a suitcase, because there's no point in buying something, trying to make your apartment feel like home, because it's never going to be your home. So for nine months of the year, you're not really establishing anything. If you were going to be there for a couple of years fulltime you'd probably rent a house and feel you're really living there as part of the country.

Jean-Pierre and Werner live their own lives away from training. I made that choice. I go for dinner at Jean-Pierre's, but he and Werner both live about 20 kilometres away.

I missed things like my nephew's birthday, which I found really tough. I missed seeing him grow. When I came back he was taller and a lot chattier.

The worst part about being away last year was that my sister's mother-in-law passed away, and both Paddy and I were close to her. I couldn't be here to hug my brother-in-law, to hug Paddy. All I could do was help them as best I could, by sending over my aroha, and offer whatever I could from so far away.

I was worried about the kids, because they'd lost Nanny, and I really understand how hard it is to lose loved ones. Sometimes even the adults are not thinking straight, because they're hurting, and trying to keep it together for the kids while organising the funeral. I would have liked to help a bit if I was there, but unfortunately I wasn't.

Those are the risks you take being so far away from home. Whenever I go away I wish to God that nothing is going to happen to my family because that'd be the worst thing that could happen to me.

At the same time they all give me love and support for what I'm doing, and they love Jean-Pierre. They just find him an awesome guy. They really appreciate what I do to help where I can, and they appreciate the work I do to be a good athlete and a good ambassador for New Zealand.

I knew that the choices I had made were the right choices, and I had to fight it to the end. When the result at Daegu in the world championships came about the sacrifice was totally all worth it. It all pays off, but I'd be lying if I said it wasn't hard making the balance.

8

To the mountain top

I've never seen Jean-Pierre Egger grumpy. Never. I've never seen him walk away from a training session angry or frustrated. He's just not that sort of person. He has that aura, that charisma, about him. It's great.

Jean-Pierre was an Olympic thrower himself, and then he coached Werner Gunthor to three world titles. He was the strength and conditioning trainer for the Alinghi team in the America's Cup, he did strength and conditioning work with the French Olympic basketball team that won silver at the Sydney Olympics, and in Switzerland he runs a lot of courses in corporate team building. His business is called Ways to Excellence.

He's a man in high demand, with his calendar filled a year ahead, so when I went to Switzerland to work with him, I knew there would be times when he couldn't travel with me to some competitions, including the world championships at the end of the year.

As soon as I arrived in Switzerland in January 2011, Jean-Pierre and I had a meeting, to talk about what I wanted to get out of my time there.

He, and Werner Gunthor who works with him, didn't take me for some dumb-arse who didn't know how to do anything.

I had the feeling of the shot and the knowledge of the event. Jean-Pierre respected that I had already won an Olympic gold and been a world champion. It wasn't like he tried to break me down and reshape me like Didier Poppe attempted. Didier wanted to turn me from a truck into a Ferrari. Eventually, I realised it just wasn't going to happen.

Nevertheless, when Jean-Pierre asked what I wanted to do, I said anything he wanted me to, and I meant it. Sometimes athletes may take things they've done in the past to a new coach, rather than starting with a clean slate.

JP reassured me that he wanted to get me as fit as possible, throwing as far as possible, but at the same time there would be a lot of hard work to do. He said, 'I'm not sure what your capabilities are.'

I said no matter how hard it was I'd try. He didn't take me from here to there in two minutes; he took his time, and worked with what I was able to do week by week. But I knew immediately it was working for me as an athlete. Everything Jean-Pierre said I tried to implement. The want to learn, the desire to be better at throwing, to advance myself as an athlete, all helped me through the year of being isolated.

From the word go, every phrase that came out of Jean-Pierre or Werner's mouth, technically, I was glued to, taking in every bit of information I was being given, then trying to do it in the circle.

I quickly enjoyed going to training because I knew I was going to be greeted with smiling faces, people who were going to be motivated and ready to go, to train hard. Because I was so connected, and wanting to improve my technique so much, I was almost like a child learning from the master.

We started with a training camp, where we found out a lot about how we would work together. He found out more about me as an athlete, and now I was in a situation where he was the coach and the boss.

Jean-Pierre is 68, but he's still pretty strong and moves pretty well, so he's able to mirror what I'm doing with lifting and in the gym. It's one thing to talk to an athlete, but sometimes it's better to be able to show them a visual, so you can say, 'Okay,' and try to mimic that.

JP doesn't talk a lot, but he'll let you know how it's going. Even if it's your first throw he makes sure you're in the place you should be. He's also very happy to praise. When you do well he's onto it. The man's a legend.

If he needs to correct something he'll ask me what I did wrong. I'll say, for example, 'I didn't get my left leg to the board enough,' and he'll say, 'Exactly, I don't need to say anything else,' and he leaves it.

He praises you for knowing what you've done wrong, and that you can correct it. With a lot of athletes, if they don't feel the throw, they don't know they're doing wrong, and the problem is hard to break. If I can find what's wrong I can work with it. We'll discuss what's happening. If I'm not throwing so well, he'll reassure me at the end of the session that not every day will you throw 20 metres.

Werner, having been a world shot put champion, a very good-looking guy and well built, you might presume would be a bit up himself. But that's totally not him. He's very quiet, quite reserved, but also very funny. He's one big gentle giant. He's two metres tall, and for someone like me, being surrounded by two big guys, hey, it's perfect.

Werner's a real homebody. He's married to a lovely woman, Nadia, and they don't run to the bright lights. He just likes to hang out with mates and play cards.

Werner's a perfectionist. He was a 22.75 metres shot-putter himself, and an astonishing athlete. At the same time that he was the world shot champion, Werner was also an amazing jumper. He high jumped over two metres, and he did hurdles. His training clips on YouTube showed what sort of jumping he did.

He had that long, fast twitch fibre muscle in his body that made it possible to jump so well. To be 130 kilos and still be able to high jump over two metres — that's Superman stuff.

Werner has a great sense of humour, but at training he's always looking for perfection. Whereas Jean-Pierre is, 'Hmm, very good, you pushed one long, but you need to do this,' type of thing, perfection for Werner is more bang, bang, bang, every 'i' dotted and every 't' crossed, every time.

I had a T-shirt printed for Werner because every time I was training, there was always a 'Yes, that was good, but . . .' The T-shirt had its message in French, English and German across the chest. He just cracked up when he saw what it said: 'Yes, but' and 'Oui, mais' and 'Ja, aber'.

Every time I throw he says, 'Mmm, oui, mais . . . you can maybe push a bit longer.' We laugh. 'Werner, you're killing me.'

Our arrangement for coaching is that Jean-Pierre sets up the programme and runs it. Werner steps in and runs it by himself if Jean-Pierre's not there. Otherwise he helps Jean-Pierre.

They have the odd discussion while I'm throwing, when they talk to each other in German. I have no idea what they're talking about and it's kind of funny for me, watching as they go back and forth. I just sit there and smile at them. Luckily, Swiss German is a little less harsh than the way Germans speak it, so it doesn't sound too fierce.

On Mondays JP usually brings in a programme for the rest of

the week, in three-week blocks. He confirms what's happening that week, how many sessions a day, what we're doing, and then he gives me the programme on paper.

We do our weight training on an indoor track, a massive facility which has a 200-metre track in the middle and a pit in the corner for the weightlifting. Next to the area is an outdoor 400-metre track, and an outdoor circle. If it's raining we have the indoor circle, which is portable. If it's nice outside we head out there.

Every morning I'll head off to training, and in typical Swiss fashion we'll sit down and have a cup of coffee, then we go on to the gym or the track. It is almost like an outlet going to training, because I get to leave my room.

In a throwing session we'll go for as long as 90 minutes. We warm up with a medicine ball, then throw for the rest of the time. Because I rarely throw a 4-kilogram shot, the weight I throw in competition, you don't take it to heart too much if the shot isn't going very far.

Jean-Pierre's way of delivering what I wanted to achieve, and his method of attaining that, were totally different to what I'd been used to. When I throw, his whole focus is on feeling what I'm doing. You may have a throw that goes miles, but if you don't feel the throw it's really hard to understand what you just did, and if you don't understand something, how can you do it again?

I didn't see great improvements in distance immediately, but feeling the throws, yes, I did, and that was the important thing. Now I fully get the feeling of a good or bad throw myself, so if the throw isn't good, and I turn around and say what I did wrong, Jean-Pierre says, 'Great, you felt it. I don't need to say any more.'

The emotional connection happened immediately, but the feeling and the understanding of what he wanted me to do technically was very hard for the first two months, actually quite frustrating. I had to try to feel what he wanted me to feel, and how the shot should fly. Once or twice in a session I would achieve it, but it wasn't as consistent as he wanted it to be.

Then, four weeks out from the world championships in Daegu in late August, boom, I felt it. Every single throw session from then on I felt what I was supposed to do. Tired or not, I still felt it. If it was slower I felt it. Just before I competed at a Diamond League meeting in Paris in early July I started to find what I wanted and so I threw 20.78 metres in Paris, which was really good. But then we peaked and we went to Daegu, and that's where everything had to fall into place. It had been a long process to get there, but we achieved it.

The most obvious change Jean-Pierre has made in the gym with me involves a specific type of training, called plyometrics, based on jumping, aimed at developing power and speed ('plyo' is the Greek word for jump).

In training now, five full-sized hurdles are placed in the gym just a metre apart, and, from a standing start, I'll make five two-footed jumps over the lot.

It wasn't something I'd had an emphasis on earlier in my career. When Didier wanted me to do it, I was too heavy, and I wasn't trained from baby level, so to speak. Jean-Pierre saw what was in front of me, and to make sure I didn't get any injuries from it, he made it a progressive thing, bounding on mats with no shoes on, trying to get my dynamics off the ground faster, being lighter on my feet, which all contributes to having a good throw.

At the start we did jumps on a foam mat, about 30 metres long, and did them side to side, double-foot jump forward, single-legged jumps, single-legged hops, lateral jumping on mats on your own, not over anything.

Then we did stair jumps. We'd jump up some stairs, which in the gym are quite wide apart and deep. Next, we did squat jumps with the bar, still not over anything, working on the reaction off the ground.

That was the extent of my jumping for several months, and then we began to slowly add in the hurdles. It took me a while to get confident. I felt clumsy at the start, but it progressed.

It has such a lot to do with confidence. I'm confident now that I'm strong enough, fast enough and dynamic enough to get over those hurdles as fast as possible. If you're not, if you're strong but you ain't dynamic, or your plyometric skills aren't good enough, there's a risk in jumping over hurdles.

Once, when I was first starting, I nearly broke a hurdle, bent it in half. I landed on the hurdle, not over it. That dents your confidence a bit.

Jean-Pierre just keeps doing what he does, training, and keeping his positivity going. 'Treat the ground like fire Valerie. Leave the ground, leave the ground, leave the ground' — and you do.

The jumping started things I had never done before. At first I wasn't physically able to do it: I was too heavy, I wasn't dynamic and I wasn't light on my feet. It hadn't been part of my training from the time I was 14. Now it's a big part. Jean-Pierre had the confidence in me that I could do it, which made me have confidence as well, made me believe that I could get it.

When you're as big as I am and you go to jump, you feel, 'Oh shit, how am I going to get over this?' But then you go, 'Okay, jump.' Boing. 'Leave the ground, leave the ground, don't go into the ground. You're touching fire, touch and go, touch and go.'

JP uses a stopwatch for the exercise. At the start, over five hurdles it was taking me three and a half seconds, now I'm under three seconds. It just goes to show how the speed and the confidence have grown.

When the jumping came up, the weights came up, too. The shot put is always going to follow when that happens.

We warm up for a session in the gym by jogging beforehand. I might do jumping backwards, then a 30-metre sprint. I jog, then stretch, do a few abdominals to wake them up, then training.

With weights Jean-Pierre is not all about the one rep max, putting everything into one big lift. He's all about doing threes or fives at a weight as high as possible, and keeping the rhythm while you're doing that.

So when you're squatting you're not going down, up, pant, pant, wait, do it again. I do 180 kilograms in the squat, down–up, down–up. To him that's more of a rhythm like I have in the shot put.

My personal bests with the weights have gone up. I did 140 kilos in a power clean and a behind-the-neck jerk, double leg support (not a split). The hardest thing in that lift is to get the weight up above your head, and if you split your legs to do that it's much easier.

I used to do snatches from the mid thigh, which were my favourites, but with Jean-Pierre I started doing them off the ground. Being as tall as I am, that's a long way for me, to lift the weights in just one movement. JP's theory with the snatch is that if you lift it from the thighs you've got quite a short movement, but from the ground it's like the shot, a long movement. I was happy to go along with it, although it took a long time to get used to it. Off the ground it's a whole different story.

His theory has always been that you have to mimic what you do with the shot in the weights room. You can bench press until the cows come home, but you must include a contrast fast bench press as well. You're not a power lifter, you're not a weightlifter; you're an athlete, a thrower.

Finally, you get into a rhythm, and we worked a lot on that in 2011. When you squat, rhythm: down–up, down–up. When you bench, rhythm: down–up, down–up. Everything now is in a rhythm.

When you throw the shot, it's a rhythm. You don't clunk, clank; it's whoosh. Jean-Pierre makes the sound effects. He goes, 'Valerie, you're like, boomp, boomp, you need to be boing, boing.' I'm, 'Oui, oui Jean-Pierre.' So when I'm jumping it's all boing, boing, boing. You're not clump, clump, clump.

In one gym session we'll do jump squats with a bar with some weights on it, holding the bar behind my neck, then squat down, jump, squat, jump. Then one minute later go twice over hurdles.

Other athletes use the gym, of course, but in most sessions it's me, myself and on the odd occasion Matthias Sempach, a Swiss wrestler. Jean-Pierre helps him out with his weightlifting.

The harder weight sessions we do together. I love that, training with someone else. The French come over sometimes for training camps, which is really good for me.

We use medicine balls to work in dynamics. I throw them over the head, shot put style, hammer style. I throw to the wall, or we have a throw at a target on the stairs. You might throw 10 throws to stairwell No. 9. There's always an objective.

They're very conscious about looking after my back. Werner's had back surgery himself, and told me from the word go that if there are any problems or pain, I have to let them know. If I look uncomfortable at all he asks whether my back's sore. You can't lie. I tell him, and we try something a little different.

We have a thrower's gainage session, which is a specific trunk session that involves abdominal work with weights, aimed at building core strength. You just kill your abs. There's also cardio gainage, where you do skipping in between the exercises, 30 seconds of skipping, 30 seconds of exercise, and so on. Sounds easy, but it's actually really hard.

Both Jean-Pierre and Werner are totally honest, and you have to be. They'll tell me, for example, if they think I need to lose some weight.

In the past I didn't really do stretches. I'd just pack my bag and see you later. I couldn't be bothered, to be quite honest. I used to be one of those eggs who just gets in the car and takes off.

Jean-Pierre actually puts it in the programme. Now I have to hop on the bike and do some cardio, and then do the stretches. It's a different way of approaching stretching. Let's be honest, stretches are bloody boring, but the thing is, by the time you feel you're tightening up and need to stretch, it's almost too late. The new regime certainly helps with preventing injuries.

Leading up to the competition, I use the cold bath at the centre. The water is about 10°C, so it's not actually an ice bath. Ice baths work for some people, but they've never done anything for me. I don't panic if there's no ice bath available when I'm away competing.

With training in Switzerland, I've had to deal with a whole different situation. It's not always easy, and it is harder because it's not your country. When I'm in Auckland I train at the Millennium centre on the North Shore, and all the staff there will go that extra mile to help you out.

In Switzerland it's clear-cut really. You just have to make things work. I had to make things work, and they have. With Jean-Pierre I feel more responsible, I feel more confident, I feel freer. He's an amazing person.

9

You have gold here

Valerie's coach Jean-Pierre Egger spent a lot of the New Zealand summer of early 2012 in New Zealand. Before he and his wife Beatrice returned to Switzerland he shared his story of working with Valerie.

When somebody asks me what the difference is between a great athlete and a good athlete, I would say it's the ability to recover energy as fast as possible. Valerie has a quality you find only in great athletes, a capability to be able, in some minutes, or a short time, to be strong, then relax.

The best athletes I have seen in the world, when they have to compete, or to work in training, they give all. When they finish, and need to relax, they can do it.

Does it seem to me that there are almost two Valeries, one fierce in competition, and one warm and friendly in normal life? No. I see Valerie as one person. I couldn't say there are two persons. To me it's Valerie, finish.

We have a harmonious relationship. In sport or in enterprise I usually have this relationship with others; it's not unique to Valerie. It is in my nature.

The way I function with Valerie is for me something quite

normal. What is special to me is that Valerie is the best woman athlete I work with.

Valerie was 16 in 2002, when I first met her, in Auckland. I had a phone call from Kirsten Hellier, who knew that I worked with Alinghi and asked if I would come to a training session with Valerie.

I didn't know Valerie, but we organised a training at Mt Smart. I remember clearly one thing I said to Kirsten, 'You have gold in your hands,' because I thought Valerie could become the best woman shot-putter in the world, if everything went well.

Why did I think this? First it's physique, and she was in great shape. She was athletic. I saw also that she was mentally strong and she knew what she wanted; she was determined. Also, she was very attentive to information.

Over the next eight or nine years I didn't see Valerie very often, but it was a pleasure to see my prediction for her become a reality.

I always kept some contact by email, sometimes about training, and later she came to Switzerland for a training camp.

After she stopped training with Kirsten, I knew about Didier Poppe starting to train with her in April 2010. Didier said to me, 'I will come to Europe,' and some weeks later he asked if Valerie could go to Switzerland while he went with Jacko to Singapore.

With Werner Gunthor we went to Zurich and we saw Valerie, and the day after the competition we met at the hotel, and we spoke about the goal of her staying at Magglingen, and what we had to do.

She came, for 10 days, and we completed around five technical training sessions. Technically, I saw the problem very quickly, what could be better. But the problem is to make it better, not to say that you see what it is.

I have my strategy, and we applied it, and Valerie's response was very fast. The next competition she was really better. She said, 'Thank you,' and she was very happy to win at the world cup and the Commonwealth Games.

The next contact was with Didier by email saying since Valerie had been in Magglingen he believed she had a problem communicating with him. The contact with her was more difficult. She had a problem understanding what technique he wanted from her.

It was very interesting to me because he said, 'What have you done?' He didn't understand what I had done that took her so much further with her throws. To me it was odd that he didn't say, 'Many thanks.' I must say by this point my response was in French, and I said what I wanted to change, to correct.

Personally, I will not try to make a problem for a coach, but instead reinforce and help the coach to train someone, not to create conflict with the coach.

Didier said only, 'Since she came to Magglingen, I have a problem.' This problem for me became bigger when Valerie phoned me a little bit later and said, 'I cannot continue to work with him. I will stop working with him, and would you accept that I come to work with you?'

It was a shock for me, because it was a big pleasure to work with her, but the problem was with Didier. He came with Valerie to me, and I thought we could arrange something to fix the problem, without Valerie coming back to stay.

I could not imagine that Valerie could leave New Zealand, because I know what the country represents to her. She loves her home, and I didn't think it was possible for her to leave.

When I saw that she was in a desperate phase of her life, I thought we must find a solution. Then, when she told me she couldn't continue to work with Didier, the decision became easier for me. If Valerie's decision was final we could try it, and see what happened.

Some weeks after that she was in Magglingen, but only for two weeks. It was in winter, not an easy time for her alone there because in wintertime Magglingen is very dark and cold. I must say when I saw Valerie in spring I realised it was possible for her to stay a longer time without big problems.

Her friend Sandra (from French athletics) came one time, two times, then her strength trainer Mike McGuigan came from New Zealand for two weeks, and then the competition season began in summer, and we began to travel, to move, and it became better for her.

Swiss people discovered Valerie, too, and it became easier for her to feel good. Swiss journalists can be very hard to please, but they did some good stories in the national papers, and she was on television. Not many foreigners have this exposure on TV and in the media in Switzerland.

We have a very open relationship. I am not an aggressive person when I coach. I know where I want to go, I have a line, I have a structure, but I am not aggressive. We must look for good human relations.

If somebody says I don't accept this, or they say I can't change, it's not a problem for me. But I know where we should be going.

I must not forget to mention that as a coach I will never wait for a thank you after each training session, but only Valerie always says thank you.

From the first, we knew I could not go to the world championships in Daegu. The planning for my work with seminars is done long ahead. I told Valerie I can make this, this, this, but in Daegu you must make it with me not there, as I could not change things.

The afternoon of the final I was a little bit nervous. We have two sofas and the TV over here in the room at my home. My wife Beatrice was on one sofa, with me on the other. I said, 'You stay there.' I had my phone because I was in contact with Sandra, and she was telling me all that I needed to know, because the television doesn't show all the event as it progresses.

Sandra says warming up was good, no problem. After the first throw was not so good (19.37 metres) I was a little nervous. But Sandra said: 'No problem, she's good.' 'Okay, I hope so.' I told Sandra she should say something to Valerie, and then after the fourth round (20.72 metres) I thought, 'Okay, it cannot be bad now.' After the fourth round Beatrice came and sat with me, and she was very happy, too.

When Valerie made 21 metres, I knew it before I saw the distance, because it was absolutely crazy. She did exactly what I dreamed for her. You can sometimes have a good competition without being very good technically. In this throw she did exactly what I wanted, and she had to throw a big throw with that.

Then, when Valerie held up a picture, Beatrice said to me, 'Isn't it your photo?' She didn't know I had given it to Valerie. It was a photo of when I qualified for the Olympics for the first time.

It was a fantastic moment for me to talk on the phone with Valerie, one of the great moments in my life. This is the goal of the coach, to make an athlete feel they can go away, and not feel that without the coach they will fail. A good coach is someone who makes the athlete confident in themselves.

When I first worked with Werner, I heard people say to him, 'When Jean-Pierre is not beside you when you are in the circle, you will not be able to perform.' My goal was to correct this idea. Very soon I sent him up against the best thrower in the world, alone. He went to Berlin, Rome. I was only with him at the world championships.

He got better. Everything gets better that way. For me it's very important. For me what has probably been a goal in my career is to coach coaches, but to do that I must be an example myself, because if I want to educate them to make the athlete independent, I cannot do it differently.

To have the athlete confident is more important than for me to be at the Olympics and to show I am the coach. Valerie is the one in the light. We help.

It's the same as we do with our own children: we find them the way, we try to do our best, we always try.

10

Reaching the stars

My coach, Jean-Pierre Egger, gave me a big envelope before I left Switzerland for the 2011 world championships in Daegu, Korea.

He told me not to open it until the morning of the final. You know what it's like when you were a kid, and you found a Christmas present before the day? I wanted to peek, but for the life of me I couldn't. I tried to hold it up against a really bright light in a bathroom, but I couldn't see through it. He'd put whatever was in there in between purple plastic sheets.

When I did finally open it, and read what he said, it gave me a real kick of confidence. I felt he believed in me and, although he wasn't able to come to Korea, he'd given me what I needed to do all the way from Switzerland.

There were three parts to the message. The big picture from him was in English. He told me to 'throw as long as you can until you reach the stars'. Next, in English, was how to reach those stars, followed by two throwing technique points, carefully explained in French.

There was also a photo of him, with him throwing, every fibre concentrated, and the comb-over he used to have flying up in the air.

Together it was the perfect way to start a day where we'd see, in the short time we had together, how far the training he'd packed in, to get me in the best possible form, would take us.

I'd been in Switzerland from the start of April and then went straight from there to Daegu, leaving three days before the competition in late August.

Mike McGuigan, who runs Jean-Pierre's programmes for me in New Zealand, and physio Lou Johnson came to Switzerland. We spent two weeks together there, training and then tapering down, to make sure we were on the right track and injury free.

Korea is in the northern hemisphere, so it was their summer, and normally it's supposed to be hot as hell, but the weather wasn't as predicted. It was raining when we arrived, which made it interesting because on the morning of the qualifying it was just as hot, 35°C, 100 per cent humidity, just sweating our butts off. It wasn't something we hadn't been competing in before, but it was a weird change when it went from heavy rain to being sunny but bloody hot.

Normally at the world champs they put you in a hotel, but this time the people of Daegu made a village for us, so we lived in a compound where they had training tracks and a throwing area. The teams lived in new apartments that would later be sold to the public.

I was the defending champion, ranked number one in the world, but none of my support staff was part of the nine-person New Zealand team. There was a manager, a physio, a massage therapist, a middle-distance running coach and a javelin coach, Debbie Strange. It's still pretty political in our sport — who you know really.

We couldn't get accreditation for Lou, but we rang a

friend, Yvonne Mullins, from Oceania, who was able to get her accredited to the Cook Islands team. Fortunately, Oceania athletes were put in the same building, so Lou and I were able to room together. Mike McGuigan was living outside the village in a hotel. Mike had accreditation to get into training venues, but he couldn't stay or have a meal with us in the village.

We arrived just before midnight, and by 1 am we were at the village and went straight to bed.

Now there were two days before qualifying. Next morning after breakfast we had a quick rub-down, then a light jog and recovery, all inside the village complex. The following day we did weightlifting, just a very light session at the main stadium where there was a better weight-training facility. It was sort of a recovery day again, light flush of the legs, check the back out, wiggle around and see how we're going.

Another person in the support group was my friend Sandra, who is a French throwing coach. Mike and Lou are wonderful experts in their fields, but Sandra knows more about throwing than Mike and Lou together. That was quite important for me, having an extra set of eyes looking at the technique while we were there. Sandra's athletes didn't qualify so she volunteered to help me out, which was very nice of her.

Despite the jogging, running, stretching, waking the body up, getting the flight out of me, and trying to get myself up for competition, I slept really badly the night before the qualifying session and I felt like crap. Jet lag had kicked in, and at the same time I was having a skin rash problem.

During the qualifying it was hot as shit and in the warm-ups I didn't feel anything great. I felt shitty with the heat, and against the leotards, against the skin, it irritates. I just had to keep my head up and do what I had to do.

I tried to get myself up, had a drink, put ice on my head. Warming up I was just, I mean *just*, landing on the qualifying mark, which was 18.45 metres. Usually, when I warm up it's popping over 19 metres, easily. This time I felt like I was trying really hard and it was only making 18.45.

When the competition started I was determined. 'Okay, just one throw and then let's get out of here.' You have three throws to qualify. So I held it together and threw 19.75 metres, to be top qualifier. Then I could pack up and get back to the village, thank God.

We caught the first bus, took a shower, lunch, had a nap, and then we all went back to training. I work best when I keep the body stimulated. Some athletes work best when they rest, and that makes them feel fresher. I actually get into a lethargic mode if I don't train and keep the muscles pumped and the blood circulating.

That night the finals didn't start until 9 pm. The three of us, Lou, Mike and I, went out to the warm-up track at the stadium. The meet was still on, and everybody was in the stadium, so there was nobody on the track or in the weights room. We had it to ourselves, and I had to do push presses. Normally, Jean-Pierre and Werner Gunthor spot me. That's when I'm on my feet, and when I lift the weights up they catch the bar at the top and help bring it back down.

So I was in the middle with the weights, and Lou and Mike were spotting. But Jean-Pierre is 1.93 metres and Werner is 2 metres tall. Mike and Lou are both around 1.54 metres.

So I'm there lifting and I swear to you they're having to stand on either side on boxes to spot for me. So I'd be lifting, get it up, 'Yep', and they'd bring it back down, all the time balancing on boxes.

We lifted well, and then I had to do some jumps. Normally, I do them over hurdles, but we couldn't find any, and we had to do them on benches. We found a steel bench, almost like a chair, and I jumped onto it and broke it in half. Luckily, none of the helpers was there so we just pushed it against a wall and did rebound jumps off the ground.

I lifted very well that night and felt so good: really dynamic and happy and ready to roll. So I knew the next night was going to be pretty sweet, as long as the next 24 hours went well, with sleep.

That night I had the best sleep ever. I was still a little nervous, though, and I knew there was a long day coming up. Usually, the qualifying and final are all done in one day, so competition fills in your time.

In the morning I went through all the usual routines, played cards with Lou, but then I did something unheard of for me: I went out of the village. I met Sandra for a coffee for an hour to help kill the day.

Then I went back in and tried to sleep, but I just found myself watching videos, tossing and turning.

At last it was time to go. About five o'clock we caught the bus, and it's about half an hour to the stadium. You have to be ready to report at the latest just before 8 pm. You give yourself plenty of time because it's not like the Olympic or Commonwealth Games where there's a designated lane for the buses. You're going with the flow.

On the bus I had headphones on and I didn't even talk to Raylene Bates, the manager of the team, who was sitting next to me. I never used to listen to music, but now I do. It actually keeps me calm and you're in your own world. When you're warming up it's the best, because nobody can talk to you.

Music is huge for some athletes, but it's not a 'God I'd better have it' for me. It's not a vital element that I'd feel lost without, just upbeat reggae music, nothing in particular. No heavy metal screaming stuff. I'd go crazy listening to that.

At the warm-up track getting ready for the final my former coach Kirsten Hellier was there with her athlete. It was an interesting time for me, because it was the first time at a world champs without Kirsten.

I had to be careful, because she knows what I'm like at this time, so I had to play my game quite seriously. I saw her and her thrower, but I didn't go up and say hello. I just left my headphones on, left my glasses on, and warmed up. You've got to do that, just play hardball, and be a stubborn cow and focus on your own shit.

Lilian (Lijiao Gong), who won bronze at the world champs in Berlin in 2009, is really sweet. She always smiles and nods, and I nod back, but that's all I really do.

Mike and Lou were very quiet because they know I'm not being disrespectful when I'm not saying much. It's just how I roll. They're great to be with. I just have to nod and they'll come and help me with whatever I need. On the warm-up track they're right there next to me. Mike can help me stretch, Lou can check out anything.

Once we'd warmed up they took us on golf carts to the first call room. I felt good physically, and mentally I was okay, so I did what I usually do, being pretty chatty in the call room.

I did have some nervousness, some butterflies in my tummy. That's normal for me, but it was heightened this time, I think, because of what happened in 2010.

This was a make or break for me. New coach, new regime, new people around me, so for my own sake, and for everybody else that was supporting me, I had to pull my head together and do this shit. I knew I had a big throw in me. It was a question of when it was going to come.

The call comes and we're off. It had been hot during the day, and by the evening it was still quite humid, which I actually like.

The tickets were really cheap, so there was a big crowd there. They were noisy in Korea, but they're not as crazy as the Chinese crowds, who go all out.

We were able to get Sandra into the athletes' stand. Lou and the New Zealand team were on the other side. If you look at the YouTube clip of the final, Sandra was the one with the glasses sitting next to Mike. She was texting Jean-Pierre and he was texting her stuff to tell me.

It's gone from not being able to communicate with a coach in the crowd to a free-for-all. The officials can take you over to the fence to talk, and then they can take you back into the arena. Sandra was able to give me tips, to stay down or whatever. All she's got to do is make a gesture. It's all hand signals. You know what's going on.

My first round was pretty shitty, with a foul. I put my foot on top of the stop-board. The second time I threw it was also a shit throw. I think I was in sixth place. The third throw was better, 20.04 metres, so I took the lead. Then they recalculate and you go into the top eight.

At that time I walk around swearing at myself. You don't need to know it all, but I don't hold back. I'm basically saying, 'Come on Valerie, what the hell's wrong with you?' But nowhere near as politely as that. If I said it to someone else they'd never talk to me again. I was hard on myself, but I knew I had it in me to do much better.

It's all about focus. In the first three rounds the German girl,

Nadine Kleinert, who didn't throw so well, kept telling me she was going to stop. I tried to be nice, so I nodded to her, but really I just wanted to concentrate on what I was doing.

Then I was the fourth person to throw and, thank God, I threw 20.72 metres.

The American Jillian Camarena-Williams came out and threw just over 20 metres, then Nadzeya Ostapchuk threw a couple of centimetres more, and she was second. They were both only just over 20 metres, but I never underestimated Ostapchuk, because in the warm-ups she was popping out 20 metres, no problem, bang, bang, bang, like she always does. In the competition there was no sign of it.

My fifth throw was a foul, and I thought, 'Shit, that was a really good throw.' It was another foot foul over the top, which is really unusual for me. So I asked them to show me a replay.

From the angle I watched it was a fifty–fifty call. It was up to the chief judge. He said it was a foul, so I lived with that.

Then I was walking around, sitting in No. 1, feeling I could do it. Once again I was counting down. No. 8 threw, didn't get past me, next, not past me, on to Jillian, and she threw just under 20 metres, so she was happy because she got bronze. Ostapchuk threw, and she didn't make 20 metres either.

Then it was my last throw. I'd won it. I knew I had 21 metres in me, and I felt on the 20.72 I had no push on it; it just came out of my hand. I thought maybe 20.30. Then I saw what it was, and it was 'Okay, let's go!'

It was so easy and so fast. The reason it went so far was that I was technically in a fantastic place in the circle. I was able to marry all parts of my body together, and off it went.

So on the last throw I was, phew, gotta push as long as possible to reach the stars.

I memorised what Jean-Pierre had written on that piece of paper. I knew it was a big one, because I reached so far with my arm.

When it feels like a perfect throw it'll go a long way. As soon as I left the circle from the back I was thinking, 'Push your hips as long as possible.' That was the only thing I was thinking of. That meant the hip moved faster than the arm. It's easier to throw your arm quickly without anything else coming through. But 60 per cent of the power is from your hips.

So I was thinking of throwing the hip, as opposed to throwing the arm. So when I threw the hip it felt like slow motion, and I let that throw go for as long as possible. I left my arm out for so long it was still out there when the shot hit the ground.

That was when I knew it was just so easy, so almost passive, yet dynamic at the same time. It was such a perfect throw. You know from the word go.

I knew it was a big throw. I thought maybe 20.90. I was walking around screaming my head off. I picked up the note from Jean-Pierre and held it in front of the TV camera, because I have so much love for this man, and I wanted to make sure he was part of my winning that night.

When it came out 21.24, the more the merrier man. I was so happy I had no voice. I'd thrown a personal best, done it at a major competition, and broken a championship record. It was the most amazing feeling of my life.

Because we were so late when we finished, by the time we'd had a drug test and done the media conference it was very, very late. I was on the phone to everyone, and it was a very happy time. Back at the village we went to the bar, but I think I had about one and a half drinks. I was so tired.

The next morning I crashed out. We went back and did some media stuff for New Zealand, then on to the stadium for the medal ceremony.

Jean-Pierre had given me some time off, a couple of days so I could go and watch some of the other New Zealanders compete and support them.

What felt so great about Daegu was knowing that this is not the end for you; you're starting here. To be able to throw so far and do this much after being with Jean-Pierre for less than a year is freakin' amazing.

11

The life

Basically, my sport is also my business. I'm a sole trader. I compete, and that's how I put bread and butter on the table.

That was really hard to do at the very start, when people didn't know who I was. At that stage if I got a couple of hundred euro I thought I was rich.

I'm like many other small businesses. I have to have managers and accountants and lawyers to make life smooth sailing. The only difference is that I'm the only one bringing in the income.

Coming from South Auckland, I grew up in a house where we had very little money. Our food budget was $40 a week.

I'm almost trying to show people there is another way of living. You can do better; it's just a matter of working hard for it. Yes, I do live a more comfortable life than what I did growing up, and that's always been my goal in life. That was my mother's goal. Your parents want you to have it better than they did. But I didn't get to where I am sitting on my arse doing nothing. I'm training, driving my body, getting operations, injections, all to succeed at what I do, to get the rewards.

People close to athletes know how hard we have to work, know what's involved. A few people might assume that we make millions of dollars and live like kings and queens.

It's totally not like that.

My niece's friend asked her whether I go shopping at Countdown or somewhere flasher. My nieces live in Mangere in the family home, and I go back there to where we lived 20 years ago, and I feel like I'm at home.

My niece's friend said, 'What's her home like? She's famous.' My niece says, 'I don't know, she's just Aunty Val.' Other kids think that because I'm a well-known athlete, and have a flash car and all the rest of it, I'm somehow different. But Sharne's just really, 'Hmm, I don't care, she's just my aunty.'

The life of a professional athlete is certainly a different way to make a living. After I'd left school I worked as a waitress, and before the 2008 Olympics I was working at Macleans College in Bucklands Beach in Auckland for 25 hours a week. Now I'm a fulltime athlete.

My first manager on the world athletics circuit was also my coach, Kirsten Hellier. That's quite unusual. In most cases they're two separate people.

Since 2010 an Australian, Maurie Plant, has done all my bookings for the Diamond League. He's the international liaison man for Athletics Australia, and has acted as an agent for years, for people like Cathy Freeman.

It's pretty much a managers' game, as well as a ranking game. You only get to compete if the people running the meet agree. If you are a champion, it's easier to get into a competition, because then you're a drawcard. If you don't have a manager, you're totally reliant on rankings. If you have a manager who has Usain Bolt, he may have Tom, Dick and Harry, who rate bugger all, may not be in the top 50 in the world, but they'll get into the race because the manager uses Usain as leverage. If they don't take the others, they don't get him.

The Diamond League only began in 2010. When I was starting out, there were grand prix events, as well as the Golden League, but the Golden League was much more restricted than the Diamond League.

The Golden League had only specific events, and the women's shot put wasn't one of them. It was usually the events that are considered glamorous, such as the 1500 metres, the 100 metres and the pole vault.

Then they swapped it to the Diamond League, where everybody gets a fair break, and in every event now there's the same chance to win the same money as any other event. In 2012 if you won a Diamond League event the prize was $US10,000. Every event carries points from first to third place. At the end of your season, if you've won the most points in your event overall, there's what they call the Diamond Race prize, which is $US30,000.

We all, bar the marathon runners, get seven or eight events a year in which to compete, including a final, where you can win double points. The meets are all over the world, from Paris to Shanghai to New York, to a final in Zurich.

Usually, you have to get yourself there, so travel costs are pretty big. I travel solo to all of these meets. The luxury of living in Switzerland is that I can usually travel with what amounts to an overnight bag.

I organise all my flights myself. There are two reasons. First, I've got a good travel agent. Second, I can choose the flights that are the best for me. If you leave it to somebody else to do it they may not choose the most direct flight, just to save a couple of hundred dollars.

I made a pact with myself after the 2008 Olympics to upgrade myself on long flights. I'd always flown economy class up until then. Can you imagine trying to fit into economy class with long legs like mine? Basically, my back can't handle it. After an hour or two of sitting I'm doomed. I need to lie down — that's the best for it. Standing up or sitting is the worst.

As soon as you arrive you're met at the airport and taken to the hotel the meet promoters have arranged. Since I've competed in the Diamond League, most athletes have had to share rooms. The luxury of being a champion is that you don't have to share your room with anyone, which has helped me a lot.

Who makes the Diamond League finals, you would think, would be done with a points system, and it is, to some degree. But to another degree managers come into it as well. There's an element of show business to it all. Some girls are not on the starting list right up until the morning of the event. Then it can get pretty bitter. If managers get their athletes in there's money to be made.

Athletics being a sport for individuals, you might think we don't have friends outside our own management team, but that's not the case. When there's a new girl on the block you say hello and make her feel welcome, even though she is your competitor. At the end of the day everyone is a human being. When you're competing you want to kick their ass, but you don't kick it all the time. You have a chat and see how they're doing.

My first encounter with senior athletes was at the world cup in Madrid, in 2002, and I was just in awe of Astrid Kumbernuss from Germany, a former Olympic champion, who had also won three world titles. She was the person who turned women's shot put from being a manly event to being a pretty, more feminine affair because she was such a beautiful woman. By then she was nearing the end of her career, but still very highly respected, and still able to throw far.

I had to have lots of respect for all the throwers because I was the newbie. I wasn't any better than anybody else. Astrid was very nice to me, and I just thought she was the best person out there. We had photos taken together, and we had a few little chats, but it wasn't easy because she spoke German and I spoke English. I didn't want to bother her either.

At the worlds I finished fifth with a personal best of 18.40 metres, the first time I'd thrown over 18 metres, and that was a big jump for me, because I didn't just get over 18 metres, I got a fair bit past it.

Not all the throwers when I started were as charming as Astrid. The Ukrainian shot-putter Vita Pavlysh was very hard in the face, with quite a tough personality, pretty much a man, and difficult to get along with. She was caught using steroids in 2004 and banned for life. I saw a photo of her when she started throwing and by the end of her career she looked quite different.

Now I have great friends within shot putting. I usually see the same girls at every meet. There are a few that change, meet to meet. It may be a local girl, or someone with a good manager who can get them in, or they need the numbers, because there has to be a minimum of eight.

I see Cleopatra Borel from Trinidad and Tobago, and Michelle Carter from America, all the time. Michelle is a good competitor; Cleo is my great friend on the athletics circuit. I usually arrive only two days before the meeting, but because you've established a relationship for so long it's easy to catch up again.

Outside the competition we get along very well. Michelle plaits my hair, does nails and makeup, all those girly things. Americans always have a big makeup bag.

One thing that has amused me on the circuit was learning how a lot of the black Americans have fake hair. They have weaves.

One day I had to take Michelle's weave out and it took me three hours. I was so amazed with it I kept doing it. It was as if someone had braided her hair and then sewn hair onto the braids. That becomes like their real hair. You have to very carefully cut it out.

Nadzeya Ostapchuk is the only one among the women shot-putters who doesn't join in. You just get a nod from her. That's it. In a dining room if you see someone you know you'll sit together. But Ostapchuk always sits by herself all the time. She chooses to be a lone wolf. She could join in if she wanted to, and be made welcome. Her nature is that she doesn't want to socialise at all. Her team-mate Natallia Mikhnevich will sit down and have a bit of a yarn, but Ostapchuk doesn't even spend time with her.

You have to wonder what's going on at home, and around her, and what her manager or coach has in mind.

Here's something very bizarre. Her coach sent me a letter when Kirsten and I split up. He said that if I wanted to get to 22 metres I should go to Minsk in Belarus and train with him. My first reaction was, 'Ah, interesting. I wonder if Ostapchuk knows about this.' I have the letter pinned up in my kitchen on the fridge.

The way I saw it, I was basically doomed if I went. I don't speak the language, I don't know anybody there, I don't know anything much about the place, but I do know the alphabet is Cyrillic, so I couldn't even work out the language the way you can with French or German, where they have the same alphabet as we do.

A fact of life for an athlete today is the requirement to have drug tests. I've been undergoing them for most of my career, but it's picked up a lot since I started winning titles overseas. I really hate the six o'clock in the morning knocks on the door, but that's what you've got to expect.

You go on a programme where for one hour every day you

have to be available for testing. You text where you are or you go online or you call an 0800 number. It can be a pain because sometimes I had situations in 2010 when drug testing didn't come into my head. I had other issues in my life.

It was difficult for me, so I had a missed test. You get a warning, and if you have three misses you are disqualified.

In three weeks I can get tested up to three times, including a blood test for EPO, or erythropoietin, a hormone that stimulates red blood cell growth, making it easier to carry oxygen from the lungs to the muscles. The blood tests are more common in long-distance, endurance sports than it is for us in throwing, so they don't take blood all the time. But they always take urine. The blood test is actually the easy one.

The test administrators just turn up. If you're going out somewhere you have to stop and do it. They knock on your door and identify themselves as testing for the agency. There's a drug tester and a chaperone who watches you. We all sit down, with a piece of paper we all sign, and they read out my rights, which I'm familiar with now.

I get the same person all the time in New Zealand, so it's at a point where if he wants to get a cup of tea at my home he can get it himself.

They tell me how much urine they want, about 90 to 100 millilitres, which is collected in a little beaker. The cup is slightly smaller than a coffee cup, so you can imagine that for a woman it's not the simplest thing in the world to do.

They offer you a drink, then we all hang around until you want to go. Then when you go to the toilet there's a routine I know off by heart now. First, you wash your hands, not using any soap. Pull your pants down to your knees, tuck your top up under your bra. Do a 360-degree turn, and sit down.

You open the beaker and leave the lid inside the plastic bag, and hold the beaker in your hand. I actually get the lady to turn a tap on, and I get her to talk to me.

Having had to do it for so long, you try to get over the stage fright of peeing on demand. But it's not the easiest thing to do. The woman is standing in front of me, looking to make sure it is going from me into the cup.

The worst thing you could do on a drug test is have a partial, not supplying 100 millilitres. If that happens they seal the beaker up, and then you have to hang around and try to go again. I make the lady talk to me, because I think it helps me relax. The most important thing is to not miss the cup.

The first time I was tested was when I was 14. Oh my God, it was so embarrassing. Luckily, I had a lovely lady who was a bit like a grandmother to me. She had water with her, she turned on the water, she sprinkled water on my face trying to make me go. Looking back, I think it was important that I did it at an early stage, because then I knew what was going to happen later on, so there were no surprises.

The people in New Zealand are pretty good. The worst one I ever encountered was in Split where the woman knelt down on her knees to look, and I was so disgusted at her, and felt so awkward, that I couldn't really go for ages.

Another bad one was when I won the world cup in 2006 in Athens. The woman was on her phone texting, and I was saying, 'Please talk to me . . . How was your day?' She just snapped, 'Good.' 'Did you enjoy the athletics?' 'I don't know.' I started yelling out and called Yvonne, our Oceania team manager, and said, 'Get this bitch out of here right now.' I pulled my pants up, stood up, chucked the beaker on the ground, and walked out. I got a lovely lady after that, an Australian.

The crucial thing is how the chaperone is with the athlete. It's not the most pleasant thing to do, and it's an awkward position for both of us really. But if they don't want to be there, don't do the job. Sometimes I think they should make all chaperones pee in front of another person so they can see what it's like.

Unless you've had to do it you don't really know what it's like. I've asked all the chaperones who have ever tested me, 'Have you ever had to do this in front of someone?' They all say no. Then I say, 'Well, try to put yourself in my position right now.'

As far as drugs go, I've never taken any of that shit and nobody has ever offered anything to me. I guess they know I'd never take anything. I'm actually very cautious about what medicines I take. Some prescription drugs look innocent, but they can be on a banned list. I think it's important to associate yourself with a doctor who's in the system, and knows exactly what you should never take. My doctor, Graham Paterson, is in the New Zealand Academy of Sport, so he knows exactly what's in the system. For example, you get a small card which lists what you can and can't take for a cold or the flu.

Everything has to be above board. You must never just pop a pill for something innocent in case it's not allowed.

The time where it can be difficult is when you're travelling. If there are language problems, you never take anything because you can't be sure what's in it. So if you do need a painkiller, or something like that, you take as much as possible with you.

I never buy anything across the counter, except maybe paracetamol. Even things like hydrocortisone creams for skin irritations can be dangerous because they have a form of steroid in them.

We now know for a fact, from files uncovered after the Communist bloc fell over, that athletes in places like East Germany were being fed huge amounts of drugs on a regular basis.

As far as making the sport drug free, my feeling is that athletics is as good as it can be at the moment. For the amount of testing that's done now, you'd have to be pretty slick to get away with it. But at the end of the day it's almost like crime in general: the criminal is always going to try to get ahead and the cops are going to be chasing from behind. There are so many weird things that can go on, like women inserting urine bags into themselves to get a clean test.

For some people there's a survival instinct kicking in. They may get only one chance to get ahead, through athletics, and they'll take something to succeed, even if only for a short period of time until they're caught. For them and their family one competition could represent five years of normal salary.

I don't think New Zealanders are seen as drug-takers in general. In my time the only real drug issue was with the marathon runner, Liza Hunter-Galvan, which I was very sad to see.

But, generally, I don't think drug taking is part of the modern New Zealand track and field culture. Nobody is suspicious of someone else doing it, and it's great to keep it that way, because we're so small and we don't have that many athletes.

If you're good at what you do here, you can keep your place without having five or six people (as you do in much bigger countries) snapping at your heels. In that case, to keep your edge, you may be tempted to do something extra. Unfortunately, some people do turn to that, but I don't think we have that mentality in New Zealand.

As a proud New Zealander I've always enjoyed being part of a team for the big meets, world championships, and Olympic and Commonwealth Games.

Even in track and field, which is obviously very much an individual sport, you do actually get a team feeling when you're at the big events. You're a very small team, and you maybe haven't seen each other for quite a while, because you're all in different parts of the world chasing competitions. You have to live in the team environment, because there's no choice, but in fact if you've been by yourself for a long time, it's nice to feel part of a group.

So when you come together there is that team unity. At the same time you have to be pretty self-centred leading into your competition, because you have to do it yourself.

Once your event is over, however, it's great to get involved, and I always support the other athletes once I've competed. In 2005 in Helsinki at the world championships I stood in the rain handing out drinks to Shireen Crumpton who was in the women's marathon. We drink-dispensers stood there for two and a half hours, but it was something I wanted to do to help where I could.

You aim to make friends with everyone in the team, and there are usually more males than females on the team. So while Sarah Cowley, the heptathlete, is my friend among the athletes, we've only been together in one Commonwealth Games team. Stuart Farquhar, the New Zealand javelin thrower, and Brent Newdick, the decathlete, are the ones I usually spend time with when we're away.

After it's all over there's always a big party. They make it clear there's a liquor ban at the village, whether it's an Olympic or a Commonwealth Games, but when it's all over on the last night Kiwi teams somehow manage to find as much alcohol as you could want. There's always a big bash at the end. How big the celebration is does depend on what's coming up in the near future, but you generally do let your hair down a bit after a major competition.

Left: Nick Cowan, my manager, and a dear friend, organised a great night at the fantastic Dine restaurant at Sky City Grand for my family and friends before I headed off to get ready for the London Olympics.

Below: Two great supporters at the Dine dinner, Murray McCully, Minister for Sport and Recreation, and my old mate, the Mad Butcher, Sir Peter Leitch.

The 2011 world championships in Daegu, South Korea were make-or-break time for me. My coach Jean-Pierre Egger gave me a note saying to 'throw to the stars'. In my last throw, a personal best of 21.24 metres, it felt like I had.

Life on the road. Some room, somewhere. Thank God for mobile phones and Skype to keep in touch with the ones you love and what's real.

In March 2012 I went to Istanbul for the world indoor championships. I wanted a good start to Olympics year, and have to admit the fact the first time Nadzeya Ostapchuk had beaten me for two years had been in 2010 at the last world indoors was in my mind, too. Winning was a massive relief.

When I won the world indoor championship in 2012 in Instanbul, my main emotion was one of relief. I just couldn't stop smiling.

At the Swiss Institute of Sport in Magglingen with my coach Jean-Pierre Egger. You hold the shot at the end of your arm, but as Jean-Pierre always says, you throw it with your whole body.

'Clean palms, dirty fingers.' Jean-Pierre is a master of shot put technique, and one aspect is that the shot should be released, not from your palm, but with a snap of your fingers. It feels wrong, but do it right and it flies.

Throwing into a clear Swiss sky at Magglingen. I can get frustrated, looking too hard for perfection. Thank God that I've never seen Jean-Pierre grumpy. Never. The man's a legend.

I left my heart in the arena in London, but it just wasn't my competition.
I went into qualifying with my nerves shattered and, no matter how hard
I tried, nothing flowed.

Jean-Pierre and I hoped we'd be shedding tears of joy in London. To be honest, they ended as tears of disappointment.

From the second I heard I'd won gold, I haven't opened the box with my silver medal in it, and I never will.

Even in the professional world there are times when you have a party, have a good time and some laughs. I think it's important, because most of the time you lead a pretty straight and narrow life.

At the end of the Commonwealth Games in Melbourne in 2006 the New Zealand team management put on drinks and nibbles, and they had so much wine and beer there it wasn't funny. The management said at eight o'clock the bar was closed. I got Craig Barrett the walker and a couple of the other guys and said, 'We need to stash the fridge in our house.'

I put four beers down my tracksuit pants, covered up with my jacket, and took them back. By the end of the function we had our fridge full and six bottles of wine as well. When the NZOC party closed down, our party opened up. We had a mock court running where you had to drink if you were found guilty, and everyone was.

In the morning I woke up with a hangover, and a moustache drawn on with a permanent marker. The table was broken, there was a hole in the wall and I had to be at the airport by 6 am to go home. Strangely, I had the best flight ever.

In order to do the work you have to do to stay competitive, you need support in many areas. Obviously, coaching is hugely important, but I'm fortunate enough to have great backing away from the track, too.

In New Zealand all my business stuff is run by Nick Cowan. He's a former athlete himself, a 400 metres runner, and Nick's been there to help me through the good and the bad times.

For the last few years I've received a Performance Enhancement Grant every month from the government. What you get depends on your world ranking. I don't like talking about money, but I fully understand why those details are made public. I get $60,000 a year.

Athletics New Zealand have come to the party a lot more in the last three years or so. They've been very good. I'm actually pretty lucky because your rankings and your results have a big effect on how your federation is going to support you.

I apply on an individual basis to Sparc for funds to help with my campaign towards an Olympics. Track and field has done quite well with those grants, because as a sport it has fared pretty well at the last few Olympics, and the payments are based on results.

The reality is I guess that Nick Willis and I can thank ourselves for that. The formula is pretty straightforward: if you do the job you will get the rewards.

Commercially, since Visa have come on board as one of my biggest partners, they've not only allowed me to do what I do but we've also developed a good personal relationship. Visa have a great crew and that makes a difference. You do go an extra mile for them. I do a lot of photo shoots for Visa, who are also an official Olympic sponsor. I shot an ad for them in Paris.

In 2012 I signed an agreement with Nike, and I've been with Mitsubishi since 2007. In New Zealand they provide me with a car which they service and look after. I just fill it with petrol. They also help me get a lease car in Europe.

Air New Zealand are on board now, too, and Sky City are also very helpful. I hosted the Sky City Christmas party for the kids from Starship, which was really fun. You try to fit it all in.

With sponsors there's always a contact person who you deal with, and if you have a good relationship it makes it much easier. The most difficult part for me is finding the time to do something. I may sometimes be tired at the end of the day, but once you're there you get into the groove and enjoy it.

For some years I've given as much time as I can to Totara Hospice South Auckland. They did a wonderful job caring for my mother and our whanau, and I was proud to accept an invitation to be an ambassador for them.

There are some people in the public eye who say they don't like being recognised. But I really think it's how you manage people paying attention to you, how you engage with people. If you're not rushing somewhere and people come up and say hello, relax and enjoy it, because it ain't gonna last forever. Once I retire and I stop throwing the shot put, it won't take long for people to forget.

You are public property, so you should present yourself well to them. For me if people want to say hello, I say hello back. If people stare, I smile.

It's hard for me to hide anyway, because I'm so tall. Sometimes people walk past and recognise you, but they don't want to harass you.

I go to the same supermarket all the time, and if people talk to you while you're pushing a trolley they're very polite, 'I'd like to wish you luck' or 'Congratulations, well done.'

Young kids are the least embarrassed. They just say, 'Are you Valerie Adams?' Or the funny one is when they go, 'Aw, you look bigger on TV. But you are tall.' I say, 'Yeah. TV doesn't do you justice, but I am tall.' They really want to say you look fat on TV but instead they say, 'Yeah, you look big on TV.' I'm like, 'Aw yeah, they say TV puts 10 pounds on you.' After all of that they usually say, 'Gee, it's so nice to meet you.'

Kids will break the ice when parents are a bit too shy to do anything. At a Breakers basketball game a kid came up and said, 'Excuse me, are you Valerie Adams?' I said, 'Yes, I am.' He said,

'Great,' turned to his dad, nodded, yes it is, then said, 'Can you sign this for me please?' He held out his little bit of paper and I signed it. He said, 'All the best for the Olympic Games.'

Children are just more open than adults. If I hear a little kid saying, 'Mum, Mum, that's Valerie Adams,' right in front of me, I'll go up and say hello.

It can make your day. I was paying for my petrol at a service station and the guy behind the counter, who I think was an immigrant from the Middle East, said, 'I salute you for what you do for our country, I really admire you.' He actually stood to attention and saluted me. I thanked him very much. You have to embrace it.

It can be really amazing. I started the Auckland marathon a while ago, and I got a letter from a woman in Devonport who said she had met me when I started the race. She said, 'I'm 68 years old, and I've never written a fan letter before. My partner and I met you and got our photo taken with you, which now hangs on my wall. We're so proud of you, and wanted to let you know that we got lucky and got two tickets for the athletics in London. If you see two people with a flag with a fern on it, that'll be us.'

I just thought how lovely it was that she'd taken the time to write and to let me know they're going to London.

I think how you treat people does depend on the field you're known for. In sport we don't get pampered, don't have a makeup room. Nobody's running round with your water bottle.

If you're home-grown, your family has given you values and you remember where you come from and where your roots are, I think that plays a big part in how you act.

12

What I learned from Valerie

Nick Cowan, a former track sprinter, is Valerie's manager, the point of contact for all commercial activities. But, as he says, the relationship goes far beyond figures on a balance sheet.

My wife Jo Harlick (at the time my fiancée) is a physiotherapist, and was part of the health group assisting the 2004 New Zealand team at the Olympic Games in Greece. Jo was staying on the same floor in the village as Valerie, and when it was time for Val to go to Olympia from Athens to compete she said to Jo, 'Hey, you're a good physio, you wanna come to Olympia with me?'

At the time I was working with adidas as their category manager, which meant that I was in charge of all products, choosing what came into New Zealand, and ordering it all. So I was on the leadership team, working with the sales and marketing managers.

When Jo came home from the Olympics she said, 'You guys have to sponsor Val. She's going to win in Beijing.'

In the leadership team I pushed for the idea of Valerie being sponsored. She and Kirsten Hellier came in to talk with me. I said, 'Here's what we can do. I know you, Kirsten, and I have a bit of interest in track and field. I used to do it, too, but I was a sprinter Valerie, sorry.'

To cut a long story short, adidas started sponsoring Valerie. There were some issues around her tracksuit for the Commonwealth Games in Melbourne in 2006, and I felt that it was important I made a real effort to make sure it fitted. It kind of did in the end.

What came from that assistance was that Kirsten came by herself to see me and said, 'I'm managing Valerie as well as coaching her, and that's not really ideal.' She didn't ask straight out, but floated the idea of whether I'd be interested in managing Val.

I said, 'Look, I would be keen to do so. It's something I've always wanted to do, but I need to check with Jo before I quit this job.'

Jo said, 'Why are you even asking me? Of course you should.'

I went back to Kirsten and she arranged with Valerie to come in and see me. The conversation from my end went, 'This is what I can do for you. I'll manage media and sponsors.' Valerie said, 'You seem alright. I quite like you. I like your wife, and she'll kick your arse if you don't do a good job for me. I'm keen.'

We went for a year without a contract. Valerie was sponsored by adidas, and there was no money involved in that contract, just clothing and shoes, so we didn't see any conflict. I wasn't getting any money from management fees from the sponsorship deal.

My job at adidas had grown to the stage where I was overseas every second week. My son Thomas was 18 months, and effectively I'd missed nine of those months. On one flight when I was coming home I thought, 'I'm managing someone who's now a world champion, and not doing a great job of that. I don't even see my kids, and I'm not being fair to my wife.' So I left adidas late in 2007.

It had became obvious Valerie was amazing and going to be a star, so I went on to manage her almost fulltime. Initially, I took on another job as well, with New Zealand water polo, but everything changed when she won gold in Beijing in 2008. I received 75 text messages in 10 minutes after she'd won, and for the next six weeks I was getting about 30 phone calls a day from the media seeking interviews, people wanting Valerie for speaking engagements, from schools wanting visits. It was the same for Valerie. It got out of control.

That was the beginning of the end of working fulltime elsewhere.

Valerie and I went through some low patches, because I wasn't keeping up, she was a big star and things either weren't being done, or they were being done at the last minute, and she's not a last-minute person.

It reached a stage where we had to make some decisions. I said I'd leave my employment, and Valerie put an offer on the table. She was really fair and said, 'I'll give you three or four months to work through it.'

Now I manage basically everything apart from the Diamond League.

Valerie's great to work for. She always does what she's said she'll do, she's a lot of fun, she wins and she's certainly not difficult to sell to people. With Valerie, you can put her in any situation. She's been sitting at a table with the global board of Visa and had them eating out of the palm of her hand. Twenty minutes later she can be with a bunch of school kids, and they're hanging on everything she says.

Valerie has a presence. She can walk into a room and not say a word and carry that room. I've seen that charisma and thought that if she can take that talent through her life, it'll be wonderful. She'll be enriched as a person, but she'll also have a great career.

I saw all that, and it made me extremely motivated to help guide her.

Valerie's a lovable person. Jo says that I manage Val, and do this and that, but at the end of the day we all, the whole family, just love her, so we want to do everything we can for her.

I've learned so much from her about high performance. She's the epitome of what you should do if you're a high-performance athlete. I competed in track and field, and went to three world champs. I've said to a few people that I wished I'd known when I was an athlete what I know now from her. I too had a great coach; I wouldn't have won a gold medal, but I would have been a hell of a lot better than I was because of what she's taught me.

What I learned was that, as an athlete, while I was never as talented as Valerie, I would have nailed what I wanted to do. I would have achieved the goals I wanted. What Val showed me was that if you really want to do it, and you do it properly, you will achieve your full potential.

When Valerie's overseas, we try to have a phone conversation, or a chat on Skype, every week. Sometimes it's to deal with things, sometimes to check she's happy with what we're looking to do, or often it's just a catch-up. There's no set time.

We used to use Skype quite a lot, rather than phone, because it's free and international phone charges can be fierce. But I've got a young family, and it's not always easy to be running Skype. Also, on the phone you don't have to look your best.

Once when talking with Val I was wearing my wife's pyjamas, which were from when she was pregnant so they fitted me. I hadn't thought about it; they were just the pyjamas I'd grabbed.

Valerie looked and said, 'Are you in pyjamas?'

'Yes.'

'They're women's pyjamas.'

'Yes.'

She puts on her 'Hmm . . . mmm . . . mm ah-hah' voice. It wasn't long after that incident that I quickly did a deal and got our phone calls funded.

When Val's in New Zealand we meet each other once a week in person. People say that it must be easier when she's away because there's not so much to do. But it's actually just as busy. Her business and life in New Zealand doesn't stop when she's overseas.

We have a cast-iron agreement, that I'm available 24/7 and my phone sits by the bed, because with the profile she has you never know when she might have to contact me.

If I have a frustration working with Valerie it's that she's underestimated in some quarters in our national sports system for what she does to be as good as she is. She's not underestimated in how good she is, or what she wins, or where she stands in her event in the world. But she's underestimated as to how she goes about getting to her goals.

Sometimes Val's methods don't match people's expectations and I have to navigate with organisations, saying to them, 'This is what she wants to do. You need to let her do it.'

In 2008 we organised a meeting for Valerie with Minister of Sport and Recreation Murray McCully. At the time she was waiting for funding, and having to pay for travel out of her own pocket, while she was preparing for an Olympic Games. Before the meeting I told Murray he'd hear some things he might find hard to believe, and he'd wonder if what he was hearing was for real. Sure enough, in the meeting he just looked at me and I said, 'I told you.' He was great in helping us shape Valerie's way forward.

With the help of others we arm-wrestled Valerie out of the system for her to be able to do it her way, so she could work out herself what she needed in order to win. She does know how to make a high-performance programme work.

In 2010 there had been the split with Kirsten, and there were plenty of negative things happening. Everything converged. Valerie needed a different structure, a different way. High-performance athletes reach a point where they move into a different realm, and need things to change.

I got phone calls where someone would say, 'I've been asked, on behalf of another person, are you absolutely certain that Valerie's training regime is right? We just want to know if she's training in the way she should be training?' I was quite angry at the time, as these queries called into question whether we had the skills to build what needed to be built.

Valerie said publicly at the time, 'I've been doing this for 12 years; I do know a bit about shot put.'

The issue for us was whether people who were running high-performance programmes actually understood what Valerie needed. My role was to make sure Valerie was separated from all that. Murray McCully was a huge help through that process.

A big change in attitude towards Valerie came, I believe, during the day and night of Thursday, 23 February 2012. Valerie went from working with kids at The Cloud on the Auckland waterfront to a large press conference in the afternoon, then to a great, warm farewell dinner at Dine restaurant at the Sky City Grand Hotel.

Some of those who'd been sceptical were in the room at Dine, and I think they finally got it. They saw that she was a pretty amazing, special person. They saw how she was able to go from being with kids at The Cloud, to handling a press conference with ease, to mixing with a select gathering. I feel there's been more respect for her since that day.

The public have warmed more to Valerie in the last year or so, too, because what we're seeing now is the real Val, Valerie unplugged.

How you appear on television has a huge influence on public attitudes. Valerie's much happier as a person now, so the real person can come out. There will be times when she's asked a question she's unhappy with. Once she would frown, or make it clear she didn't appreciate it. What she does now if she's unhappy with a question is she smiles, which is a brilliant way to deal with it.

We do prepare some things that Val will say when quizzed. Before Beijing we decided that we would never mention the word 'gold'. She would always say, 'I'm going to give it everything, and hopefully the result we all want will come out on the day' or 'There are never guarantees, but I'll be doing everything I can, and we'll see what happens. You can only control so much.'

She won, and that's beautiful, but leading up to the Olympics in 2012 I suggested: 'We can't avoid talking about gold this time. The public would wonder if you were taking the piss. Let's meet it head on. Let's put it out there, but take the public with us.'

So Val moved it up a notch, with: 'I really want it, and I'm going to do everything I can to get it.' She faced up to it, saying, 'Of course I want gold, but I've got a lot of work to do. I just want to do everything I can to get it.'

Basically, a briefing for a press conference is very straightforward: just be yourself. Sure, some of it is planned with Val, or by the two of us, but people do see her now as she really is. She's much more comfortable in public than she has ever been.

The great thing with Valerie is that whoever she meets or whoever gets to know her will warm to her.

We signed with Toyota before the Olympics and the head of the public relations company involved said to me, 'Just as an aside, I was in the Pakuranga night markets one day last year, and Valerie was there with her little nephew. We didn't say we knew who she was, but we just got chatting with her and she chatted back. She was such an amazing, engaging person.'

That's something that makes her so special.

13

Walking in the rain and riding elephants

Ten years after competing in my first Commonwealth Games, in Manchester in 2002, I got to see a video with commentary of the women's shot put on YouTube. I had to laugh at what they were saying. It was so very, very British. 'A bright future indeed for this young lass from New Zealand, a young giant with much ahead of her.'

It's quite amazing sometimes to get to listen to commentary, because when you're competing, of course, you don't hear any of it. To be fair to the commentators I was very young in Manchester, just 17, and pretty nervous about what was an intense competition for me at the time.

The Commonwealth Games are unusual, not noticed a great deal in many parts of the world, but very interesting to New Zealand and to the other countries that compete. I really enjoy them. To be honest the Commonwealth Games hadn't meant a lot to me when I was growing up, because when they'd had the last Games, in Kuala Lumpur in 1998, I was only 13.

But going to the 2002 Games did feel like a bigger deal than the world juniors in Jamaica, which I competed in two weeks before I went to Manchester. There was a much larger team at the Games, and it was the first time I'd ever been in a team with other sports involved.

At the world junior championships in Kingston I won with a throw of 17.73 metres, which would have won gold in Manchester. I then flew from Jamaica to England. At that time in my life I checked out the world shot put rankings online quite a lot, and I knew I was ranked third in the Commonwealth going into the Games.

Most of the rest of the team was already in the village in Manchester when I arrived, but I was in time for the formalities. I wasn't in New Zealand for the build-up, or able to fly with the bulk of the team, because I was off to Jamaica, but I was able to go to the opening ceremony. I did the whole nine yards, got all dressed up and did the waving to the crowd thing.

At that age you have no real idea of what it's about until you go to your first Games. All the netballers I'd seen on TV were there, people like Linda Vagana, Vilimaina Davu and Irene van Dyk, so I was kind of star-struck. I've got a photo of myself with Irene and Vilimaina.

The Commonwealth Games is really the only time when people from the different sports have a chance to get to know each other. We don't see each other much at all otherwise. Just being part of it was one of those 'Oh my God' moments in your life. Walking into the dining room, with people from all parts of the world, and seeing so many people in the black New Zealand uniforms walking around was really cool.

In the dining room it's like being a kid in a toy shop, only instead of Transformers, it's food. Everything is free. There are salads, meat, breads, fruit, chocolates and you can eat as much as you want. The catering in Manchester was probably the most amazing of all the Games that I've been to.

When I'd first arrived in the village I had to get into the time zone, because there was a six-hour time difference between Kingston and Manchester.

In training I actually sprained my ankle slightly two days before the competition. I clipped it in a throwing session, so when I competed it was well taped.

Qualification was pretty straightforward, and I finished top of the qualifiers.

It had been raining like crazy two days before we competed. But when we got to the final it was beautiful. The sun was out, just an amazing evening.

The Nigerian thrower, Vivian Chukwuemeka, who was 10 years older than me, took the lead, throwing 17.26 metres. I'd been consistent, at around 17 metres, and then she threw a big one, 17.53. I threw after her, and improved to 17.45, and that was the final result. Johanna Abrahamse from South Africa was third, on 16.77 metres.

Vivian was as strong as hell. I think she was benching something like 120 kg, and my best then was probably about 72 kg.

Looking at the old YouTube footage in 2012 it's quite remarkable to me that I compete exactly the same way now as I did 10 years ago. I still get that mean 'Don't eff with me' face on I had then. I'm still in the zone. Still concentrating on what I'm doing.

It was a great competition. Straight from winning a world juniors to getting second at the Commonwealth Games. At the medal ceremony I was on the podium, watching the New Zealand flag go up, loving the moment, and finding I was taller than Vivian even when I was standing one level down from her.

There were some really cool photos that were published afterwards at home. There was a lot more coverage of the Commonwealth Games than there was of the world juniors. Being young I had a pierced tongue, with this big orange ball in my mouth.

The world juniors overall were of a higher standard through the field in my event, but the Commonwealth Games were different for me because there were so many older women competing. I was the youngest in the shot by quite a lot.

It was a big learning curve, and I think I've been quite lucky in the fact I could go from world youth, to world juniors, to the Commonwealth Games, to world championships, to the Olympics. I didn't have to jump from world juniors to the Olympics.

My shot put competition was in the middle of the track and field programme, so I was able to see some other events and other sports. After I compete I will always go and watch the other athletes. I've volunteered to be at the drinks station for the marathon runners. It's really fun.

We went and watched the weightlifting, which was awesome because I was able to see Nigel Avery win gold in the over 105 kg class for New Zealand, and I was at the netball final, which went into extra time before the Aussies sneaked in against the Silver Ferns.

At the track I watched our hammer thrower, Phil Jensen, getting a silver medal, and Tasha Williams in the final of the women's hammer. I also watched Steve Backley, the javelin thrower from England who was the reigning world champion. Confession time, I was taking photos of his bum, because he was a bit of a glamour boy in his field. Hey, I was young okay? I just got into the whole atmosphere of the Games.

I went out to watch Craig Barrett in the 50 kilometre walk in the rain, where he won silver. It could have been really embarrassing, because I nearly took out the guy who won, Nathan Deakes, from Australia, with an umbrella. By accident, I swear, not on purpose. It was all just great.

Manchester was also my first real introduction to big partying. After I'd competed, and watched everybody, I disappeared for three days to party with people from other teams like the Tongans.

In the village they had a walk of fame in canvas, stuck on the ground. They put all the medal winners' names on it. So I sneaked out in the middle of the night and cut out the shot put area, the gold, silver and bronze, rolled it up and took it back home. It's at my house now.

Fast forward four years, to Melbourne in 2006, and it's all different for me, because now I'm ranked No. 1 in the Commonwealth by a long way. We were in Melbourne for three weeks before the start of the Games. It was as hot as hell, but the general atmosphere was very good.

My goal was to win, but my biggest goal was to beat the Games record of 19 metres, set by the Australian Gael Martin at the 1986 Games in Edinburgh. Without being complacent, I was confident I'd win, and happily I threw 19.66 metres, so I got the record as well.

After I'd won, I was pretty excited, but then straight away the Australian 400 metres runner John Steffensen won gold, and so the crowd lost interest really quickly in the women's shot put. It was like quick polite clapping then, okay, now pack your bag and bugger off.

I didn't go to the opening ceremony, but I stayed to the end, and was at the closing ceremony. For me the Commonwealth Games don't have the tension and pressure that the world championships or the Olympics do, and I have the chance to enjoy myself after I've competed. There was a big track and field team in Melbourne, including friends like Sarah Cowley and Rebecca Wardell, so you could hang out with people you knew. Once again I found the netballers a very humble, cool group, and easy for me to relate to.

In 2010 the Games were in Delhi in India. I'd come back to New Zealand from Europe for two weeks, and then we based ourselves in Singapore for two weeks, before flying to Delhi.

There was a lot of controversy over the Delhi Games. There were stories suggesting the Games village would be a disaster area, and that the venues wouldn't be finished in time. I actually think we made a bigger deal than needed to be made over the village. Every Games has teething problems, it was just that their problems in Delhi were a little bigger. But they were always going to go ahead with it; you just had to accept the way it was going to be.

They operate differently, that's all. For example, we had a small electrical problem in the New Zealand quarters, and one guy turned up. Then he went and got five guys, who went away and came back with 20 guys. That's how they work.

A lot of top athletes didn't want to go to India, because they were worried about getting sick. My attitude was: to hell with that, I want to go and experience this shit. I loved India because it is so different. You go to Melbourne or Manchester, and basically it's like New Zealand. But go to India and, oh my God, it's so different.

I'm not saying the village was perfect. We weren't able to drink the water, and you even had to clean your teeth with bottled water. When you had a shower it was pretty gross. The water felt pretty yuck just showering in it.

The rooms weren't really finished, there was sawdust in the corners, and some curtains broke when you pulled them across. In our laundry when you walked in there would be workers sleeping on the floor. You had to lock your doors because people were stealing things. But, then again, in a very poor country, if there was stuff to steal people were going to be tempted.

The track and field stadium itself, when you saw a picture on TV looking down on it there appeared to be a lot of dust everywhere, over the track. I'd have to say the toilets were disgusting, they stunk and didn't flush properly, and using them wasn't easy. Let's just say you had to flush in stages.

The food wasn't that flash either, but it was okay and basically safe. They had the same Australian firm who catered in Melbourne doing the food. Despite the precautions a number of the team suffered from 'Delhi belly', but I didn't get a stomach bug. I guess I'm lucky to have a Tongan tummy — stomach of steel, which you need in India.

The shot put competition was over fairly quickly. We didn't have qualifying, because there were only 12 entrants. My best friend among the shot-putters was there: Cleopatra Borel-Brown, from Trinidad and Tobago, a 19-metre thrower.

To be brutally honest, we basically knew what the standings were going to be, and I took the training I'd had in Switzerland in September, and just carried on for three weeks to Delhi. I threw 20.47 metres, which was good, because it broke the championship record again.

The day after I competed I did a lot of media, and then I had three days before the Games finished. We'd been told we weren't allowed to leave the village once we'd competed. We had to apply for leave to go out. But if you'd stuck with that you would never really have got to see the country at all.

We had been able, on an officially organised trip, to go to the Taj Mahal, and I got to pose for a photo on the Princess Diana chair where she had the famous photograph taken. But I wanted to see more.

I organised with Cleopatra to go to Jaipur, five hours by car, to ride elephants. The trip cost around 500 rupees. So, five in the morning, Miss Adams gets out of her bed, sneaks out of the village, jumps into a car with Cleo, and we drive for five hours, with no real idea where we are, seeing monkeys on the side of the road and cows just lying in the middle. If I come back in a second life I want to be a cow in India. You just rule the roost, walk wherever you want, eat food wherever you are.

Then we stop, and, being India, there's always a middle man, and they say we'll pay this man, and he pays another man, and he pays another man, and the last man gets the least money, but he provides the service.

So we start riding elephants around, which was really cool. Then we got back in the car, went and had great Indian food, fabulous delicacies, the real India.

In the car again there was a touch of *Slumdog Millionaire*, with kids knocking on the windows, begging for money. The driver just said, 'Don't look at them, don't make eye contact.' It was really sad, but we did what he said.

Then we went to a sari shop, and I tried on saris and bought a great purple one. By the time we got back to the village it was 11 pm.

I walked past the bar where all the Kiwis were, making sure I looked relaxed and innocent, and then the chef de mission,

Dave Currie, walked past, and casually asked how I was going, what I'd got up to during the day. 'Nothing much, just a little shopping in the village.'

With my bag full of Indian stuff, I got back to my room, dropped my bag and breathed a bit of a sigh of relief. Got away clean. Nobody had known we'd gone, not even the New Zealand cop who was a security man for us at the Games.

There are a lot of things in India that are tough to see. People using the side of the road as a toilet, kids scrambling through rubbish tips for food. But despite all that there's a liveliness and a real energy there. Jaipur was just amazing, so beautiful. You have to try to look past the ugliness and see the beautiful things that are there.

14

The public face

It matters to me how I'm portrayed in the media, because it's how the public perceives you and it affects how the public is going to judge you.

I've tried to put out that 'what you see is what you get'. There will always be plenty of photos of me with a serious face, because when I compete I'm fairly sombre. But there are also photos of me out there poking my tongue out and playing the fool, because when I'm not training hard or throwing I always see the humour in life.

On the one hand it is very important to protect your image if you can, because this is your livelihood. Sponsors get on board, and they want to be involved with someone who is well thought of. But there's more to it than the commercial aspect. I feel that I'm also representing New Zealand in the public eye, not just my own personal image, when I'm out in the world, so I do believe I have to be seen to be behaving in a decent way.

Basically, I had to learn how to deal with the media on my own. There's no handbook you're given on how to deal with an interviewer when you start out in sport, especially if you're just a kid who's still at school. The first interview I ever did was for our local free newspaper, the *Courier*. I was very young, a kid from South Auckland, who was never going to give anything other than really simple yes or no answers to whatever I was asked. Sometimes there was a variation, and instead of 'Yes' I'd say, 'Yes, good.' No explanation, no background on what had happened, no babbling on about the competition. Pretty much 'Yeah, good, Mum and Dad, good, thank you.' Very basic.

I was still at school, just 14, the first time I was interviewed on television. I think *60 Minutes* did a story where they came to my high school and I threw the shot, competing against three First XV rugby players. We were all in school uniform, and I had long hair. That was my first exposure to TV, and they were pretty kind to me, very reasonable. Mind you, they did go straight to the blunt questions, 'How tall are you?' 'How big are your shoes?'

That's fair enough I guess. I'm not the average-sized person. You're an innocent child at that age, and you just give straight answers.

I don't tell lies now when I'm interviewed, but I can explain things: the how, why and where. Or I can make a joke of it. Back then, it was 'Yeah, I can't find any shoes.' 'So what size are your feet?'

God, it was so strange to see myself on television. My first reaction was 'I'm so ugly.' You see yourself differently on TV from seeing yourself in the mirror. Over the years when people do see you, if there's a remark it's always 'You look fatter on TV.' I always get that.

It was bizarre for me to see myself on TV, and even to look at photos that were clipped out of the paper. I still have them now. When I was starting out I had hair so long it was down to my butt. Now I'm not fazed by it. You do get used to it.

The more time you spend in sport the more your confidence

builds, along with having a better knowledge of your sport. You travel a bit more, you learn, and you're not so afraid to express yourself in public.

When I was still a teenager, it was a little easier because I was doing so well all the time, so I had a pretty golden run in the media. I won the world youth championships, won the world junior championships, I was in the public eye, but it was all positive. Two weeks later in Manchester I won silver at the Commonwealth Games, and the stories were 'Valerie Adams, only 17 years old, wins a medal'. It was nothing but positive, all the time. Everyone liked what you did, talking about this new talent coming through. Maybe people expected my results to be always the same: getting better and better.

The first time I struck something negative was in 2004 when I went to the Olympic Games.

Let me give you some background. The Olympics, of course, are huge. I got an Olympic solidarity grant to go to the Games, and I believed some of my financial backing in the future would depend on how well I performed.

Then I got appendicitis, and had surgery just four weeks before the Olympics. So I had to get it together in a rush. I could fit in only one competition before the Games. I tried everything I could to prepare. I walked every day, as soon as they said I could, feeling like my belly would fall out. I did every bit of the rehab they told me it was necessary to do. I could have pulled out altogether, but I decided to carry on and do the best I could.

I was really young, not as strong as any of the other girls. I was a big girl, but I was a child, competing against grown women.

Being at the Olympics was a breathtaking experience. Living in a big village, seeing all these famous people like Yao Ming, the Chinese basketball player who's 2.29 metres (7 ft 6 in) tall, so everyone else just comes up to his hips. When you're 19 and you're looking at people like him you're just awestruck.

At the time 18 metres was a hard mark for me. The qualification mark was 18.50, I think, and I qualified with 18.79.

I was there with all the build-up and the high hopes, and I'd qualified for the final which was just a few hours later.

The shot put event was held in Olympia, where they held the ancient Games from 776 BC to the fourth century AD, some 320 kilometres from Athens. Getting into the stadium you walked past the ruins of the temple of Hera, where the Olympic torch is lit that today is carried in relays to the opening ceremony of the Games.

It was a very special event, even if you weren't a teenager at her first Olympics. To keep the ancient feel they didn't put up temporary stands. They limited the crowd to 15,000 spectators who sat on grass banks overlooking the arena. We competed during the day so they didn't need to erect any lighting, and they placed temporary circles in the arena.

I went into the circle, and I was crapping myself, but at the same time I was so happy that I'd made the finals at my first Olympic Games. My God.

I had three throws and I was out. My first throw was 18.56 metres, the second I fouled, and my third throw was 17.93 metres, not good enough to get me into the top eight.

I was nervous as hell, and I didn't have competition fitness, but I thought I did okay, considering. I was upset because I'd wanted more, as you do, and looking back I guess I was a little angry with myself, having hoped for more success in the competition.

Four of us were now eliminated, and we packed our bags.

Normally, in a big stadium there's a long walk around the stadium before you get to the mix zone where the reporters are waiting. But at Olympia it was so small you walked only about five metres to the mix zone.

I had so much adrenalin running through my brain. So many people had travelled up from Athens to see the event. The chef de mission was there; it was full on. I thought I'd let my supporters down and let myself down. Looking back, I shouldn't have felt like that. I should have felt proud and happy. But in the emotion of the moment I didn't feel that at all. There were only two ways I knew to deal with those feelings, to either cry or be very defensive.

I didn't know how to suppress those feelings. One of the things that does make you a good competitor is wanting to do well so badly that you get angry when you don't do as well as you believe you should have.

So I walked around, churning inside, and TVNZ's European correspondent, Lisa Owen, was there, and she asked me what I felt was a stupid question. Remember, I'd fouled the second throw.

Her first question was, 'Second throw. What happened there?'

I looked at her for a few seconds and said, 'My business, not yours.' She didn't say anything, and after another gap I said, 'It's just a timing thing, a little bit wide, but hey.'

Nothing in the interview got better from there. I didn't actually swear, but it was pretty blunt.

I know it was a negative response to the question, but really all I wanted was 10 minutes to compose myself. Would it have been better if I'd asked for a little time to get ready to talk, or she had offered me that time? Of course, but hindsight is a beautiful thing. In the heat of the moment I cried my eyeballs out, and what I said just came out of my mouth.

I had never been in that situation before, and I think, in my defence, it would have been better if she'd come out with a different question.

In all there was a negative reaction to the interview, and then, something which was pretty galling, the next day the girl who won, Irina Korzhanenko, from Russia, was disqualified for testing positive for anabolic steroids. I finished eighth overall when she was put out, and I would have had three more throws without her there. Unfortunately, that's the way sport can go sometimes.

As it turned out, I learned from the whole experience the hard way. I'm glad it happened, because it made me grow up, knowing the sort of pressure you're under when you go to the Olympic Games.

There were so many high hopes for me, but I'm not sure the media took into consideration that I was 19 years old, I was inexperienced, anything could have gone wrong, and I was dealing with getting over appendicitis.

After the Olympics, at first I think the attitude towards me was fairly tough. Before then, looking back, I'd usually been treated with kid gloves. I was just a teenager; many knew I'd lost my mother, so they had some sympathy for me. Most media were really nice to me.

After the Games, media people could be tough with me sometimes. I think there was an impression I was getting too big for my boots. I can recall feeling that when I got back, and I was explaining how I wished I'd been given a little more time after the event.

With time I've become a lot more at ease in dealing with the media. Even before the 2008 Olympics I can remember doing a press conference and I wasn't as comfortable as I was doing the same thing in 2012.

In general I guess I'm a lot happier in myself, with my set-up, in my own life, and I'm able to let that actually come out with reporters and in front of the cameras. In 2008 unfortunately that wasn't the case. I painted a lot of pictures in those years, and I painted them in the last years of my marriage to protect myself and my ex-husband.

Now I feel free. I'm a lot happier and generally content to talk to anyone. It's no big deal, it's all cool.

I don't mince my words, and if I feel I need to be straight at times, I'm going to be straight. But being more relaxed means I can also joke about things with the media. Before the meeting in Christchurch at the start of 2012 there was a press conference, and a reporter asked me what distance I was going to throw. It's a foolish athlete who answers a question like that; you're just setting yourself up for a fall.

So I just smiled and said, 'Distance is for me to know and you to find out. Everything else is a personal thing between me and my coach.' Then I said, 'I can't tell you my tactics man. I might have to kill ya.' We could all laugh then.

I generally do try to show people who I really am on and off the field, on and off the camera. I can't get to know everyone personally and closely, but I think I've been open enough to give out what people need to know.

In the media world there are people who I truly trust, and who would be called if we felt there was something we needed to make public. On the other hand, there are some who I would never talk to, and would never give an interview to, because of things that have happened in the past, when I felt badly let down. In the end you do have the option of who you give your time to.

I do try not to rush to judgement. First impressions are not always right. In 2010 I was at the Sky City children's Christmas party, and a guy was there who I'd thought was a real plonker. He was waiting for me to come out so he could talk to me, but I wanted him out of my face. Yet when we talked I found he was genuine in what he was trying to ask, and I came to like the guy.

The majority of the media people, in fact, are pretty good, and I have formed some excellent relationships.

The internet, with its numerous bloggers and critics, is worth keeping away from, or at least not taking too seriously. You realise that at the end of the day you're not going to make everybody happy, and I've reached a stage where I don't let negative people get me down.

You just have to make sure that you respect yourself, present as good an image as you can, try to show who you really are and let people make their own judgements from that.

15

Giving everything a go

Valerie's first major sponsor was Visa, and she remains an ambassador for them to this day. Sean Preston, the manager of Visa for South East Asia and Australasia, explains how a straight-shooting woman from South Auckland won hearts in the bespoke-suited world of high finance.

Ian Jamieson, who was my predecessor, was invited to the Halberg Awards as a guest of the New Zealand Olympic Committee in 2007 and at that stage Visa had started its preparation for Beijing, which would involve Team Visa.

During the dinner Valerie won Sportswoman of the Year, and then the Supreme Award. It was clear to Ian that this shy, humble girl had captured the audience on the night, that she could capture the hearts of all New Zealanders, and that she had a good medal chance in Beijing.

A few days later the relationship was officially sealed.

When I first met Val I was a client of Visa, and I met her at a couple of their events. What struck me was that she was meeting corporate people, who wouldn't naturally be the people she'd want to hang out with. What made her shine, even in the early days when she was still quite shy, was how genuine a person she was, with a huge heart, who respects people, and can quickly get on a wavelength with them.

She's a very intelligent person, with a quick wit. You see how she also really thinks things through, which I'm sure is a reflection of why she prepares so well, and achieves so highly in her sport.

Valerie has the ability to charm any group she deals with. One night at a client function at the Hilton hotel in Auckland there were rapid-fire questions for her and the phrase 'smash the crap out of it' was used four or five times, to everyone's vast enjoyment. Would it be fair to say that it's not a phrase you'd usually hear at a Visa client function? Yes. But everyone was more than happy to make an exception in this case.

Sarah Eglinton, our marketing manager, has been with Valerie at a lot of her appearances, and a thing that's impressed her is how Valerie is always prepared to give anything a go. That willingness to try anything almost came to disaster in Paris when we were filming the commercial we ran leading into the London Olympics.

Valerie was careering down a cobbled street on a pushbike, and a crazy Frenchman started driving his Citroën up the alley. He was just a paint layer away from running her over.

Andrew Craig, who works with Valerie on the public relations front, says that she doesn't just go through the motions in whatever she does, whether it's at a photo shoot or the genuine enthusiasm she has when she's meeting clients.

She gets people to open up, and in the process they have a good time, and she does, too. It takes a really special person to be able to do that. We're 100 per cent behind her, and that certainly continues after the London Olympics. There was some initial negativity in the media after London, but we know that Val will move on. We're very proud of her.

16

Heavy implement chick

Shot put is an event where you cannot cheat on what you do. You must be dynamically onto it all the time. What you put into the throw is exactly what you'll get out of it. Sometimes in the discus the wind can pick it up and help you. The wind has no effect on the shot. It's all up to you.

All your effort is concentrated into a circle with a 2.135-metre diameter. Take two big steps and you're across it. The area is very compact.

From the time I start moving in the circle until the shot leaves my hand is less than a second. At an Olympic or world championships you're putting hours, weeks, years of training into less than four seconds of throwing, so there's no room for error.

The shot is a difficult event to master. The technique might look pretty straightforward, but it's all down to subtle movements, which makes it frustrating but also fascinating.

The very first technical aspect I learned, after I first threw the shot as a 13 year old, was that you actually have to push the shot, not throw it. I guess a lot of kids learning the shot think they throw it, but it's really more like a punch or a hard push. You can actually rip your shoulder joint, even tear it from your socket, if you try to throw it like a cricket ball.

I started shuffling across the circle instead of gliding when I did my first shot at school when I was 13. Just shuffled across the circle and hoped it'd fly a long way. The big difference between me and other kids was that I was naturally quite strong, and I was always quite a big girl, so it was always going to go further than everyone else's.

But I didn't know how far I could go with it. Initially, I was getting my satisfaction just from the result. It was definitely not a feeling thing, although you do very quickly feel the difference between a throw and a punch, if you've got a good punch behind it. But the end result was more important than the feeling. What I do today is fifty–fifty. I still want the results, but now I'm also fascinated by the process.

Wherever I was throwing as a kid, whether it was a school championship or a club meet, I mostly liked getting the bigger distances out, 12 metres, then 14 metres, and I thought I was just shit hot throwing it that far and beating everyone. What came up on the board was what mattered.

I was way overwhelmed when I went to world age-group championships as a 14 year old. The throwers were all a lot older than me and had been training for much longer. Basically, my nerves got the better of me. Another Kiwi, Victoria Lowrie, was there with me, and she got into the final, finished eighth, so she beat me, whereas I'd always beaten her in New Zealand.

As a raw newcomer, just starting, I remember scraping to get to 12 metres, when the Chinese girl who won, Mei Hong, was throwing over 15 metres. I do remember looking at her and seeing how much more advanced her glide was than mine, how much stronger she was than me and how fast she moved across the circle.

I think after the world champs I started to fall in love with the shot. Learning to throw the implement became interesting to me, and I liked the individuality of it. At the same time I didn't love it enough then to give up everything else.

After Mum passed away was when it really hit me that this was what I wanted to do. I could see my potential on the rise when I was 16 years old at the national championships in Hastings, and I won the senior women's shot, and I was pretty happy with that. I threw over 16 metres, and it ranked me top in the world for an under-18 thrower.

At that point I wanted to see where this could take me. School became less important to me.

Once you start reaching some good distances, you begin to want to know what other girls around the world are doing. I used to sit on the IAAF website a lot, checking out what they were throwing in the rest of the world. When it came up that I had the potential, maybe even to win, at the next world youth championships in 2001, I thought, 'Let's do this,' and that's when I really buckled down and trained for the next year.

As a kid I had the chance to throw the shot, the hammer and the discus. They're all related somehow, good footwork, fast feet, a lot of strength needed, push the hips in and throw. I wasn't too shabby in the hammer and discus. At one stage I held records in the under-18, under-20 and senior shot, under-18 discus, and under-18 hammer.

After a training session with the shot I'd go on and throw the discus and hammer, which meant I wasn't, at a very young age, just going down one narrow channel, which I think was a good thing, because overkill could come sooner rather than later.

I also loved the discus, but the implement is way too light for me. Let's be honest, I'm definitely a heavy implement chick.

With the shot, at first I was throwing with my arm only. Slowly, as you get better you start to use your legs. Your arm is only 10 per cent of the work you have to do. That's all it is. Everything comes from the pelvis and the trunk and the feet. The arm is basically just what finishes the job off for you.

You have to remember that the strength isn't coming from how fast your arm is going. That's the easy thing to do. The arm is just the finishing touch. The strength is coming from your body, and that's where you need to be doing the work. At times I forget that. You can be so frustrated that you get, let's call it, the throwing equivalent of premature ejaculation.

As time goes by you start to learn the different techniques. In a country like Germany, where you have one head coach, they all glide the same. But there's room inside the event for differences. They have different ways of gliding, where they start, how they're positioned in the middle.

On the day we compete, once you're out there they give you a minute from the time your name comes up on the board to when you have to throw. When I step into the circle I take a few deep breaths, and look out to a point further than where I want to throw, visualising where I want the shot to land.

I go to the front of the circle, and then take two steps back, so I have my back to where I'll be throwing. I begin with most of my body weight on my right foot, then I crouch down with the left arm slightly out to maintain balance, to keep my body over the back of the circle as much as possible. It's almost like a lever.

I shake my arm over the back of the circle, and then when I start the glide I slide across into my pelvis and trunk, with my right leg penetrating the power through. At the same time my left leg comes into the stop-board, transforming the power through my body. That power finishes through my arm, with my fingers pushing as long as possible.

I come up onto my toe with my right leg, and at the same time my left leg comes in, as I go to glide back across the circle, with most of the power supplied by my left leg.

The aim is to get across the circle as fast as possible, making sure that your upper body stays down. Imagine yourself gliding through a tunnel. There's a roof over your head, and you've got to keep under it. At training Jean-Pierre makes an awesome sound effect, a whooshing sound, to remind me what I'm doing.

You want to keep the right leg under you as much as possible, have a strong position in the middle, then push the left leg into the stop-board. At that moment what you're doing becomes like a pole vault. Your left leg is the pole and your right leg is the athlete. You jam the left leg against the stop-board, and then the hips and the pelvis move through. The shot starts at the side of your neck, then it opens up and your arm comes through to finish.

A good throw is always an easy throw, it just shoots out of your hand, almost floating, because you're not trying so hard with your arm, you're giving your body the time to work through the throw.

A very good saying I've learned is 'Clean palms, dirty fingers'. If you try to leave the shot on your palm and try to push it from there, it's very hard. The aim is to have the shot resting on your fingers, with an empty palm, so that when you go to throw you get a last flick of the fingers. If it's in your palm, you lose that last snap.

It takes time to get a feeling for that, because it's hard to get a heavy implement on your fingers, and then think how you're going to flick it. In fact it feels stronger in your palm, but you don't get what you think you would.

Everything does start at the very beginning of the throw. If you're not dynamic and propel off the back as much as possible and get yourself into a good position, with your left leg straight into the board, it's pretty hard to finish off the throw well from there.

One asset I have is that I'm generally a fairly good finisher. I have that little bit of psycho about me, so in a competition I punch the shot out as far as possible regardless of what's happened with the glide. I just go for gold.

If the thought flashes into my mind, 'Shit, I didn't do this part right,' I still think, 'Let's just finish.' Some shot-putters step out, or they just sort of let the shot go out of their hand. There will be the odd time when I'm able to get the shot a long way even if my back leg's a bit too wide, so you keep it rather than deliberately foul.

For me it's a timing issue. I can start like crap, and look like crap, but there's always hope you can come through.

For some reason my fingers separate when I throw, and the shot naturally comes out of just three fingers. Strictly speaking, it should be coming off all four fingers.

The first year I was in Switzerland a young coach from France went to Jean-Pierre and said, 'I think there's something that can be improved with how Valerie releases the shot. She always releases with three fingers as opposed to four.'

Jean-Pierre had never commented on it, because I think if there was a problem, I'd probably have been the one to say, 'My fingers don't seem so good.' JP came to me and said, 'This guy's told me you use only three fingers.'

'Yeah, I know that.'

'I never knew. Do you feel anything?'

'No, I feel no different.'

'Okay then, we don't have to change. No problem.'

I'm not going to change just for the sake of it. It's the way I throw.

It's the sort of thing you would pick up with video analysis, but Jean-Pierre and Werner Gunthor never did a lot of that. I think if there was something technical they couldn't agree on they'd sometimes go to video analysis, just to work out exactly what was happening, to see if they needed to correct it, and how to do that.

We don't do a hell of a lot of video analysis now. Maybe once every two months, if that. With Jean-Pierre the focus is all on the feeling.

My mental training, however, does include watching YouTube video of my best throws. I've watched the win at Daegu in the 2011 world championships hundreds of times. That's my visualisation, something I do on my own, which Jean-Pierre expects of me. It's what I want to happen every time I compete, so I train my brain to see and know what I have to do. How that shot flew.

I've always been able to switch on and switch off when I'm competing, right back to the days when I was a school kid playing basketball.

A few times my sister Paddy actually had to tell me to ease off, because I'd start blocking girls, the same age, but half my size, and I was so aggressive. I put my heart and soul into it. I can't help it. If I'm competing, I'm going to compete. Paddy was the same.

When Paddy and I played together we were called the Twin Towers, and we played so well together. For me, when I was playing basketball I was playing to win.

I think it runs through the whole family. The Adams brothers were known to be aggressive when they played basketball.

When I moved to Switzerland to train with Jean-Pierre there were some big changes in how things worked. An obvious example was that my first coaches, Kirsten Hellier and Didier Poppe, always stood to my left side while I was in the circle. JP, right from the start, always stood at the back of the circle. I asked him why he did that. He said, 'Because at the back I can feel the throw with you. At the back I can feel the shot put. I can feel exactly where the shot is placed.'

Jean-Pierre is very good on technique, and as an athlete I now understand what he wants me to do. He has a real ability to feel a throw with me, from the second it leaves my hand.

I may throw in training and say, 'Aw shit,' and he raises his eyebrows and says, 'Why shit?' It may actually have been not too bad. Sometimes as an athlete you judge every throw by the distance and forget about the technical work. If I throw, he'll often say to me, 'Everything was fantastic, except for one thing. What was not optimal?'

When I was with Didier we drilled for Africa, all day, every time, all the time. Drills are like shadow boxing for a fighter, you do all the moves in the circle, but you don't have a shot in your hand.

Didier would tell me I was a champion driller, but my theory is that I can drill until the cows come home, but I need a shot in my hand, so I can throw.

With JP when we're in the circle we throw. All the other work he wants me to do is in the gym. The only thing we'll do in the circle that doesn't involve a shot is that we'll take a bar, and put it across my neck, and work the trunk, work the hips, work the pelvis. Next, it's in the front, and finishing off with a bar above my head.

We work off lighter shots, heavier shots. When you have a 5-kilo shot in your hand, it's 25 per cent heavier than what I throw in competition. Five kilos holds you back and you have to work. You have to push 5 kilos that much more, and I always feel good throwing the 5 kilos.

But while the 5-kilo shot will make you work harder, it's actually more difficult to throw the 4 kilo or the 3 kilo correctly, because everything moves faster, so you have to get your hips, legs, everything moving the way they should.

Give me a lighter shot, and it takes me two or three sessions to get used to it. I've always been a strength person, but I'm gradually getting into the habit of throwing the lighter implement at a faster rate. If you can get the two together, 'bang', you'll be pretty sweet. At the end you've got to meet in the middle.

Five-kilo shot putting is specific strength training for throwing the shot. You couldn't get any more specific. You can go to the gym and bench press heaps, do squats with this, that or the other, but if you want to build up strength for throwing, not weightlifting, throwing 5 kilos is perfect. It's totally tuned in to your event.

We still do a lot of work in the gym, working hard on getting the best out of the pelvis and trunk and making use of my stature and strength. If you train well in the gym it shouldn't put too much stress on your body when you're throwing.

I work a lot on improving the flexibility in my hips. The iliotibial band is a strong fibrous tissue that runs from your hip down the outside of your leg. When you're blocking and smashing into the board on your left-hand side the IT band can get worked up sometimes and almost seizes up on you. Time in the gym has helped ease the problem.

Now I'm older I do have a better feeling for the event. Jean-Pierre has made me understand more about what shot putting is all about, and the feeling you must have for a great throw.

I'm at a point where experience, feeling and understanding for the event allow me to analyse what needs changing during an event.

In 2011 I threw 20.78 metres in Paris on my own, and in Daegu in August, when I threw 21.24 metres for the world championship I was also on my own. I put it down to great coaching, and the confidence instilled in me by Jean-Pierre. I know what makes me tick, I know what I have to do to throw well, and, of course, I try my best to do it.

The Rising: Valerie's Personal Bests

Age	Throw	Date
15 years 3 months	15.72 m (NZ Under 18 record)	26 Jan 2000
16 years 4 months	16.11 m (NZ Under 18 record)	23 Feb 2001
16 years 9 months	17.08 m (NZ Under 18 record)	15 Jul 2001
17 years 8 months	17.54 m (NZ Senior record)	2 Jun 2002
17 years 9 months	17.73 m (NZ Senior record)	18 Jul 2002
18 years 5 months	18.91 m (NZ Senior record)	21 Mar 2003
19 years 4 months	18.96 m (NZ Senior record)	29 Feb 2004
20 years 5 months	19.32 m (NZ Senior record)	12 Mar 2005
20 years 11 months	19.62 m (NZ Senior record)	13 Aug 2005
21 years 3 months	20.20 m (NZ Senior record)	27 Jan 2006
22 years 11 months	20.54 m (NZ Senior record)	26 Aug 2007
23 years 11 months	20.56 m (NZ Senior record)	16 Aug 2008
25 years 6 months	20.57 m (NZ record)	27 Feb 2010
25 years 11 months	20.86 m (NZ record)	4 Sep 2010
26 years 11 months	21.24 m (NZ Record)	29 Aug 2011

Compiled by Roy Williams

17

Throw to the future

Track and field isn't one of those casual, social sports. I like that fact. There's nothing better than going out there to compete to win, and it's a real competition.

Basketball, touch, rugby, you can go out and have a friendly game with your mates, your family, with kids, at any level. With track and field you just can't. You cannot have a friendly hurdle race or a friendly throw-off.

Track and field is a very individual sport, where the only ones who succeed are the ones with the hunger to do so. Going to training is very boring when you're younger. It's not as much fun as a team sport can be, where you've got mates to hang out with after training and all the rest of it.

But I actually like the solo element in athletics, the challenge of trying to be the best you can be in a sport that's in 300 countries around the world. In New Zealand it's a very minor sport, but in the rest of the world it's the most competitive sport out there.

If we could harness the talent I see in Pacific Island kids in South Auckland we could be the world powerhouse in throwing, the way New Zealand dominated middle-distance running in the 1960s and 1970s. I could walk around South

Auckland right now and find 10 people who could be better than me. From a physical point of view there are kids with natural raw talent, no shoes on, throwing the shot 12 metres.

These kids can do it. Give them an implement, ask them to chuck it, they'll throw it a long way. As far as true but undeveloped talent goes, it's all out there.

Pacific Islanders aren't really built to be runners. Little white skinny boys can go out and run for miles and miles, that's their thing, but that's something most of us can't do. We're just too big. But we are just naturally strong people, almost built for sports like rugby and throwing. What's missing is being taught how to be dynamic and using technique as well as strength. Coaching is the key.

Socially, I think it's very difficult for Pacific Island kids to be involved in track and field. It's not cool, it's a lonely sport and you don't hang out with your mates.

It's very expensive, too. You're expected, because you compete as an individual, to pay entry fees, to find your way to a competition. When you're in a team event, the whole team travels, and if you can't get a ride yourself, you'll find someone to take you there.

You need to be made welcome. So much depends on how you're treated. Brown kids are very shy, and it's very easy for them to be intimidated by an older white person. Track and field is very much run by Pakeha in New Zealand. That's the reality of it.

In my own case it could have turned the other way when I first went to a coach, Russ Hoggard, in Papakura.

At first I was very put off. There were other brown kids in the squad, but nevertheless it was still quite daunting for a young brownie from Mangere to go out into the big world and

203

interact with a white coach in a sport I had no background in.

The other thing you get concerned about as a kid is how you look, what they're thinking when you do the exercises. You have to remember they were a bunch of sprinters those guys, and I was the only little fatty in the group trying to do sit-ups.

But Russ was very encouraging, and after a couple of weeks I warmed to him and I was fine. Russ believed in me, and let me join in with his group. We went running and did exercises, and used medicine balls, like sprinters do.

He kept me going. It was as if he saw something in me, when I needed someone to keep me interested, to keep me going until someone who could teach me throwing came along. Russ was the one I'd train with every Tuesday and Thursday night for an hour and a half.

He kept me in the system, because I think if there's a cut in the rhythm, it's really hard for someone to pick you back up, because in track and field it's a case of you having to go and ask. They don't come to pick you up.

From a very early stage, too, I wanted it so bad, so I kept going. Rain, hail or shine I still hopped on that train and went there. At that age it's not easy. I was already big, too big in my mind. Just to make sure I never forgot that, on the train to Papakura they made me pay an adult fare because they thought I couldn't be only 14. I had an ID card from the Southern Cross Campus, but that wasn't good enough for them. Those bastards on Tranz Metro, they owe me so much money, because it's $1.70 return for a kid, versus $3.70 return full fare. Mum and Dad didn't have that much money to pay extra for a damn train.

Thank God at the other end Russ Hoggard was very nice to me. I believe he wanted me to do well.

You want to put the kids on the right path, hook them up

with the right coach. But you have to look for that spark in their eyes and find something there. If you look for that spark, if you see something special in a certain kid, take hold of it and get them on the right path. It may be a hard time in their life, where Mum and Dad can't afford shoes or something like that. If you get in there and support them it can make a world of difference.

Looking back, I was fortunate enough to have had a phys-ed teacher, Teena Tugaga, at intermediate school who took me to a sports shop and out of her own pocket paid $150 for a pair of branded shoes to fit me.

That was the trigger. I thought, 'My God, you believe in me that much you'll spend that out of your own salary to buy me shoes.' Mum and Dad couldn't buy me shoes that cost that much. Tina saw something in me, I felt her love and support and 'boom' — off I went.

The first thing is to find the kids who want to do it. Only people who really want to get involved are going to make the effort. You could pay a kid all the money in the world to train every day, but if they don't want to do it, they won't. I put up with it because I believed there was something there for me. I wanted it so bad.

Track and field in New Zealand is a sport that relies on volunteers and we don't have enough coaches in general. If we made moves to have more coaches in our community, we would progress so much more. You need experts who can show kids how.

When there's no leadership or coaches involved, even for someone who really wants to do track and field, it's very easy for them to go somewhere else, to league or basketball, where there's a coach available.

When I started there were lots of runners. Beatrice Faumuina was around, and so was the javelin thrower Gavin Lovegrove, although he was towards the end of his career. But all the noise was about runners.

Four to five years into the bigger competitions I still felt there was no real recognition that we'd reached a stage where we were as good as or better at throwing than at middle-distance running. It almost felt that you had to beg, to say, 'We were great at middle distance running, and we're still great at it in some cases, but we are better at throwing now, and we're performing in the throwing area, as opposed to the track.' I think the officials have come around to the idea that we are strongest in throwing. Things have improved as time has gone on.

There was a minimal level of support for athletes when I was a teenage thrower. Zilch. Absolutely zilch. The dropout rate was high. Back then as a 14, 15-year-old kid there was virtually no help. When I look back at my first world youth champs the only two who really carried on were Sarah Cowley and me, out of a dozen or so athletes.

Money now comes out of Sport NZ and High Performance NZ to help run the sport. When you go to world championships, if you do well and win medals the IAAF helps fund that country. There's a lot more support today. They have coaching clinics and training camps.

And they're a lot more hands-on in throwing now. I've pushed the cause a bit myself, knowing that there's a lot of potential in New Zealand, working to make it work.

So in context Athletics New Zealand isn't doing too badly. The results we get at the top level do feed down the chain as Sparc is able to give us more money. I get my share for my campaign and others get a share. They're able to have national coaches and have a head of javelin, a head of shot putting and so on. They never used to have that. There are programmes set in place. There are more athletes now going to world youth and world juniors than when I was there. So that's good.

The next step will be working on retaining people in the sport. The biggest place where we lose them is from Under 20 to senior. Under 18 to Under 20, that's okay; things are better at the junior level. But it's a totally different game into the seniors. That's where there are still problems today.

I firmly believe success at the top level does breed belief, and successful athletes are an inspiration to others to get involved and work hard.

I'd love to see us present athletics in the way they do overseas, making it exciting for spectators, which in turn fires up interest among promising athletes. Germany, for example, is a country where shot putting is a national event. It's absolutely amazing. I love to compete there, because they take the presentation of athletics to a whole different level.

In the shot they bring the people so close to the circle it becomes like a little mini stadium. You're in your own little world. It feels so good. The people are screaming at you. You're not going to get people hurt. A shot doesn't fly off like a golf ball or a discus.

They do the same stuff with the javelin, right up next to the runway. You have people clapping from the sides, from the back. It's thrilling for everyone.

As a result they eat, breathe and sleep track and field every day. They get massive crowds. Some little village smaller than Waiheke may get thousands and thousands of people driving there for a meeting.

If our officials saw how the rest of the world does it, they'd change. I don't think we've quite grasped how track and field can be presented.

It doesn't have to be elaborate. A great thing in Australia is how before an Olympics they set out the qualification marks. It's a big hype, and people really get into it.

I'd love to throw a personal best at home. I want people to come up close, to be where it all happens, where you interact with the crowd, and the crowd is booming. When you think about it, you can do anything when you're presenting a meeting, and the only limit is your imagination.

Wouldn't it be great to have a throwers' meeting in New Zealand where you didn't charge too much, maybe made it five bucks, and it became viable for the public to support the athletes? It doesn't have to be at a traditional stadium. I really hope that one day I'll be able to throw in an event at The Cloud on Auckland's waterfront. Wouldn't that be a buzz?